Advanced Praise for
THE MELODY OF MARRIAGE

"I love your book! One of the first tests when I look at or review book is "Would I buy this book?" For *The Melody of Marriage*, the answer is a resounding Yes! Keep swaying to the music.

Bob Dickinson
Veteran Media Executive, Christian Author and Social Activist
Author of "*Me, Jesus, a Beer and a Cigar*"

"We love the backbone and foundational references to King Solomon and Shula. . . the interweaving of personal experiences and testimonies while providing R&B and Spiritual song headliners."

John W. Fowler
Executive in Procurement Services
and
Trudy Fowler, Educator
Spiritual Leaders and Motivators

"Cynthia D. Jones gives us a beautifully authentic portrayal of marriage that is both earthy and honest yet wonderfully inspiring. She shows us that the normal struggles don't have to overshadow the beauty and romance for which we all long. She creatively weaves in some of the great music and gives us practical guidance from Scripture to keep our marriages renewed and growing. I recommend this great book for newlyweds as well as those of us decades into this mysteriously wonderful union."

Anne Irwin
Founder of One Hundred Shares

"...an excellent tool for young and old couples to strengthen, renew and refresh their marriage."

Mark and Marilyn Townsell
Spiritual Leaders Married Over 40 Years

"We highly recommend this devotional experience for married couples of all ages."

Roosevelt and Renita Quick,
Marriage & Relational Coaches
Co-authors of *The Power of Agreement: Biblical Principles for Maximizing Marital Fulfillment*

"A great blend of real love stories, biblical principles, and guidance on how to build a thriving marriage that will endure and improve with time."

The Waltons
Jesse Walton, Jr. SVP, Financial Advisor Morgan Stanley, and Spiritual Wealth Management Leader
And Angela P. Walton, Founder & President of Breakthrough Marketing

THE MELODY OF MARRIAGE

A Musical Journey Through the Song of Solomon to
Invite Couples to Grow in Christ, Connection,
Communication, and Commitment

THE MELODY OF MARRIAGE

CYNTHIA D. JONES

The Melody of Marriage: A Musical Journey Through The Book Of Song Of Solomon to Help Couples Grow in Christ, Connection, Communication and Commitment

Copyright © 2022 by Cynthia D. Jones
Foreword By: Quentin Jones
Published in Cumming, Georgia.

ISBN: 979-8-9863919-1-4 - Hardcover
ISBN: 979-8-218-00917-5 - Paperback
eISBN: 979-8-9863910-0-7 – ePub

Library of Congress Control Number: 2022910252

Published by: Walking in Victory Ministries2, LLC.
Printed in the United States of America

Internal Layout and Design: InSCRIBEd Inspiration, LLC.
Edited by: Shiwana Rucker, Cynthia D. Jones, Penda L. James, Cynthia Tucker
Cover Art: Soleil Branding Essentials www.soleilbrandingessentials.com

All real-life anecdotes are told with permission from actual parties involved and recorded to the best of the author's recollection. Names, in some instances, have not been used at the request of the individuals referenced. In some cases, parties mentioned are deceased. Details of some instances have been slightly modified to enhance readability or to ensure privacy. Any resemblance of any other parties is purely coincidental.

All rights reserved. No part of this book may be reproduced or transmitted in any form, electronic or mechanical, including photocopying and recording, or held in any information storage and retrieval system without permission in writing from the author and publisher.

THE HOLY BIBLE, NEW INTERNATIONAL VERSION®, NIV® Copyright © 1973, 1978, 1984, 2011 by Biblica, Inc.™ Used by permission. All rights reserved worldwide.

Holy Bible, New Living Translation copyright © 1996, 2004, 2007 by Tyndale House Foundation. Used by permission of Tyndale House Publishers Inc., Carol Stream, IL 60188. All rights reserved. New Living, NLT, and the New Living Translation logo are registered trademarks of Tyndale House Publishers.

Scripture taken from the New King James Version®. Copyright © 1982 by Thomas Nelson, Inc. Used by permission. All rights reserved.

Scripture quotations marked MSG are taken from *The Message (MSG)*, copyright © 1993, 2002, 2018 by Eugene H. Peterson. Used by permission of NavPress. All rights reserved. Represented by Tyndale House Publishers.

Scriptures marked KJV are taken from the KING JAMES VERSION (KJV): KING JAMES VERSION, public domain.

ACKNOWLEDGMENTS

I give all praise, gratitude, and honor to my **Heavenly Father** for loving me and blessing my life beyond anything I could have imagined. **Father God, You** have so enriched my life with my husband, best friend, lover, priest, provider, and protector over our home-my Boaz, Minister Quentin "Q" Jones.

It has been a joyful journey to be side-by-side in all of what life encompasses with my **Q**. I couldn't have dreamed up or created a better husband. **Q,** your support, encouragement, example, and prayers have made me a better and more confident woman in every area of my life. I love you. "Let's Stay Together" by Al Green continues to be the melody of our life.

I'm thankful for **our children, Justin and Brittany.** Your passion for grinding out life together is a testament to living your life as a united force. Your strength and determination to safeguard your marriage are admirable. May you continue to serve the Lord with joy and gladness.

To **my extended family of Intercessors, Prayer Warriors, motivators, mentors, encouragers,** and those who flat-out pushed me to complete this book, I thank you. **Angela Walton, John and Trudy Fowler, Pastor Tavares Stephens, Eddie Johnson, Owerri**

Washington, De Kelly, Reverend Dr. Michael McQueen (who called me out from the pulpit), L. David Harris and Kathy Lamar are a few of many over the years who kept believing I could do this even when I stopped writing. I thank God for **Kristy McCarley** who trusted my skills enough to allow me to be one of the first writers for her blog, Shazzy Fitness.

I have to give special appreciation to **Beverly Williams**, my special Sister-in-Christ, who has skills! Thank you for putting in long hours to help me with proofreading and editing.

Bridgette Rooks, you have been a great support to develop my brand and web presence.

And, of course, thank you to **Penda L. James, my Scribe Coach and publisher, who**, when I showed her some of my material, said, "Ms. Cynthia, you have about eight books here!" I love the relationship we have developed as you have patiently mentored me.

I'm excited to finally be "stepping out of the boat" to see where the **Holy Spirit** leads me on this writing journey.

"You are altogether beautiful, my darling, beautiful in every way. You have captured my heart, my treasure, my bride. You hold it hostage with one glance of your eyes, with a single jewel of your necklace. Your love delights me, my treasure, my bride. Your love is better than wine, your perfume more fragrant than spices. Your lips are as sweet as nectar, my bride." (NLT)
~Song of Solomon, 4:7, 9-11a

CONTENTS

FOREWORD – "I FOUND LOVE" xi
INTRODUCTION xv

Christ 1
Let's Stay Together 7
Endless Love 13
Falling Like Dominoes! 19
Heaven Must Have Sent You From Above 25
Face It All 31
Signed, Sealed, Delivered 39

Connection & Intimacy 45
Ain't No Mountain High Enough 51
Let's Get It On 57
My Girl 63
The Best of My Love 69
You Know How to Love Me 73
When I Come Home To You 79

Communication 85
    What's Going On? 93
    Can We Talk?.. 101
    I Heard It Through The Grapevine 107
    How Sweet It Is To Be Loved By You 115
    When Somebody Loves You Back...................... 121

COMMITMENT 127
    Stay Together... 135
    A House Is Not A Home 141
    Never Too Much 149
    Fortunate.. 155

Concluding Thoughts................................... 161

Activities To Enhance Your Melody............... 165

FOREWORD – "I FOUND LOVE"

Forty-five years ago, the LORD allowed me to marry a woman that changed the trajectory of my life. At the time, I was young, impetuous, mercurial, confident, and deeply in love. I wanted to marry the woman of my dreams – Cynthia. In my young mind, the next level of love had to be marriage. I had no clue what being a husband really meant in terms of my role or responsibilities; however, I was willing to learn that process with my fiancée.

My interpretation of love was viewed from a worldly perspective. In the embryo stages of our marriage, Cynthia shifted my paradigm on what love really is and what love is not, because she demonstrated through her actions what *"unconditional love"* represents. She loved me spiritually, physically, mentally, emotionally, exclusively, and sincerely! I knew she had my back regardless of the circumstances we were facing. She was a *"ride or die"* wife before that nomenclature became as popular as it is today.

She always had the doors of our home open to demonstrate hospitality and kindness regardless of where we were living. She consistently sends birthday greetings, Christmas cards, celebratory graduation cards, donations, etc., to friends and family to express her love.

Cynthia displays her love for God through her faithfulness to reading and studying His Word, regardless of how late we may have returned home from a night of partying while living in Cleveland, Ohio. She demonstrated her love for others when she volunteered to teach illiterate adults how to read and delivered meals to senior citizens through Meals on Wheels.

I found love when I witnessed my wife raise our son and shower him with motherly love, compassion, tenderness, nurturing, discipline and understanding. I watched her sacrifice for his well-being, and if that wasn't enough, I listened to her intercessory prayers for our son and for me throughout our marriage.

The melody of marriage was present when Cynthia showed me selfless love in caring for my mother when she moved into our home with the early stages of dementia. She never complained or asked for assistance. Instead, she humbly, willingly, and selflessly loved my mother during the most difficult time in her life, and I will be forever grateful for the godly woman she is! *The Melody of Marriage* will teach you and your partner how to grow in Christ, Connection, Communication, and Commitment using the Song of Solomon as its foundation.

Q

BeBe Winans' song "I Found Love" expresses my sentiments for my wife, Cynthia. Baby, when I found you – I found true unconditional love, and for that, I'm eternally blessed!

INTRODUCTION

My husband and I share a mutual love for music: R&B, Gospel, Soul, Jazz, Old School, and of course, Motown! Music has been a connection point—source of love, laughter, joy, and romance in our marriage. It has also been a stabilizing force bringing spiritual peace in the hard times of our relationship and in life in general. Music has run parallel to the ebb and flow of our marriage through many seasons.

Throughout history and in nearly all cultures, music has been and continues to play an important role in society as a form of communication. Music is good for the mind, body, soul, and marriages. If you allow the music to work its rhythms, it has the potential to calm your spirit, revive your soul, or soothe what's ailing you. It can help blend the harmony of peace and inject joy into your lives. It's also been a blessing to have Gospel Music as the soundtrack of life experiences throughout our marriage.

We are Motown born and bred. Music has ministered to our deepest woes, allowed us to celebrate victoriously, joyfully, and it enhances the mood when we want to share intimate times. We love to praise dance, exercise to music, and when it's time to enjoy good old "get-out-on-the floor" music, we engage in "raise-the-roof" dancing! And, of course, we love slow dancing to Earth Wind & Fire, Luther Vandross, Chaka Khan, Jeffrey Osborne, the Isleys, and others. That makes us grateful to God for choosing us as a couple.

Why Melody Of Marriage?

Melody of Marriage invites married couples on a musical journey through the book of Song of Solomon. The intent is to help you as married couples grow in your relationships. You will learn about Christ's love for us all and how He wants you to enjoy a vibrant relationship that honors His design for marriage.

Song of Solomon is a love song in the Bible composed of five parts (canticles or hymns) attributed to Solomon. It describes his love for a beautiful maiden, a Shulamite from the tribe of Shullam. The story goes from dating to a passionate courtship to an intimate look at their marriage. So intense was their love that she describes it as a love that's "strong as death."

Just as they grow in their connection, communication, and, commitment so can we as couples while enjoying the backdrop of music through the "Melody of Marriage."

An Example of Love

Melody of Marriage is a tribute to one of the greatest love stories in the history of the universe – King Solomon and the Shulamite woman. While some believe the Song of Solomon is an allegorical song of God's love for His people, I believe it is a love song that depicts the intensely passionate love of a man and a woman who found love in a complicated love story. The Shepherd/King finds his true love – a maiden in the fields of her family's land, which quite possibly were in the vineyards and pastures of Solomon's father, David.

The maiden and the King establish and nourish a marriage that has been chronicled for all eternity. We never know when or where we will find love, but when we do, may we cherish its intensity and intimacy with the same passion as the King and his Shula "Always and Forever!"

I have been asked, "Cynthia, is your book a devotional or a book of short stories?" To be honest, I would say that it's a hybrid of both and I will let you decide as you turn the pages. You will discover four themes in the book: Christ, Connection, Communication, and Commitment. At the beginning of each section I will share the story of Solomon and his bride. Each chapter has stories that are pertinent to each theme.

The Melody of Marriage entreats you to celebrate love as God-ordained. God's manual, the Bible, has a special book presented as a gift for married couples – "Song of Solomon," a full eight chapters on Romantic Love. Read it, embrace it, and experience perpetual freedom to express love to each other in your marriage.

Cynthia D. Jones

MOMENTS OF REFLECTION

At the end of each pillar, there will be moments of reflection that you as an individual, couple, or even small group can discuss. It is an opportunity to share what interested you and what made you think about how you can improve your relationship. What can you do to enhance and grow your marriage to take it to the next level of enjoyment and satisfaction? Commit to spending some quality time sharing your thoughts, pulling out the Word of God, and reading through scripture to see how God has instructed us to live as married couples.

THE MELODY OF MARRIAGE

CHRIST

Song of Solomon 1:1-3:5

"My beloved is mine, and I am His."
~Song of Solomon 2:16

While Song of Solomon does not mention our Lord God's name specifically, we see His presence throughout the pages of Song of Solomon. If the first part of the Song of Solomon (1:1-3:5) had a subheading, it would be called "Adoration." Just as Jesus adores His children, we read in Song of Solomon the passionate love story of a man, Solomon the Shepherd/King, who delights in a beautiful maiden, the Shulamite woman.

    Some theologians believe that the Song of Solomon is about God's love for His people Israel. Others say this is the story of Christ's love for His Church—God's love story to humanity. Yes, we are God's "Treasured Possession." Yes, He does love us with an everlasting love. And yes, His love for us is unquenchable, as Shula describes love when she says, "Flood waters can't drown love." In Song of Solomon 8:7, Jesus' love for us is unconditional and eternal. He proved that by conquering the grave to have an eternal relationship with all who receive His gift of Salvation. Our Father God gave His Son, Jesus, King of Kings, and Lord of Lords, to die for our sins. "While we were yet sinners, Jesus died for our sins" Romans 5:8 (NIV). He hung, died, and was buried, but rose from the grave so we could, in turn, live our lives and be forever with Him.

For *Melody of Marriage,* I will focus on the more contemporary translation of the Song of Solomon as one of the greatest love stories of all time between a man and a woman. The Shepherd/King Solomon finds the One who stole his heart, his "Treasured Possession," his "Beloved Dove."

Our Lord cares about every detail of our lives. We don't always have to see the manifestation of His power in miraculous healings, floods, fires, or lion's dens to know His presence is evident throughout the Bible and in our lives. He came so that we could have life and have it most abundantly. We are His greatest creation. He desires for us to be joyful and satisfied in every way.

There is nothing prudish or shameful about intimacy in married love. Satan's tool is to keep us from finding satisfaction and unity, God's blessings in a godly marriage. Song of Solomon teaches us how to love each other totally, intimately, and completely as married couples. Isn't that just like our loving Father - every good and perfect gift comes from God!

While researching, reading commentaries, and writings on the Shulamite, I had more than a few questions to ponder. Was she Pharaoh's daughter? Was she Abishag, David's former concubine? Was she Solomon's first true love? And for a man so experienced in women, what was it about this Shulamite maiden that captured his heart? Was she truly a "dark but comely" maiden from the vineyards who genuinely won his heart?

    I don't know, and I don't think there are conclusive answers. One thing is for sure, if this is a metaphor for how our Lord loves us, I'm grateful for His sacrificial, undeserved love that I can pay forward in how we all can demonstrate love to our spouses.

"The best thing to hold onto in life is each other."
~Audrey Hepburn

Al Green helped start our romance off in 1972, and we are still going strong.

LET'S STAY TOGETHER
Al Green

"How beautiful you are, my darling, how beautiful! Your eyes are like doves."

"You are so handsome, my love, pleasing beyond words!"
~Song of Solomon 1:15-16 (NLT)

Back in 1972, when Q and I first met, he was the quarterback of the football team and captain of the baseball team. He was also popular, tall, dark, and handsome walking the halls of Cooley High School. (My humble husband did not want me to write about him so explicitly).

I was a short-lived cheerleader after breaking my wrist and I ended up in the hospital. Q came to the hospital to visit, and we soon began dating! Unlike the Shulamite, I was not so confident when I met Q. I was quiet, smart, and a new Christian. Neither did I realize my beauty nor my worth, but Q noticed. Soon my light began to shine, and my confidence increased because I was loved not only by my newfound Lord and Savior but also by the tangible evidence of His love for me through Q. I believe it was by God's plan that we found each other. We decided that our song would forever be—"Let's Stay Together" by Al Green.

King Solomon was the wisest man to live during his time. He was also the wealthiest and most respected man in all the world. On top of that, he had a harem of over three hundred concubines and seven hundred wives!

I will never understand how someone can keep up with the needs, emotions, desires, and feelings of more than one spouse, but I know one thing for sure, "Shula" was his choice. She was "the fairest of all in the King's eyes."

Before you go off on a tangent, yes, Solomon was a bit of a womanizer, to say the least, with all the women he had. And this is not an excuse, but the Bible reveals that many of his wives were given to him in trades, alliances, political agreements, or business deals, and he had rare contact with them. Can you imagine trying to remember their names, let alone birthdays?

For Solomon, his lady, his crème de la crème, the one who stole his heart was the lovely Shulamite maiden. Shula was a maiden who worked the fields of her family's land or perhaps the fields of King David and was inherited by King Solomon. Her brothers took advantage of her and worked their young sister long hours in the hot sun. Hence, her skin was darkened by the sun. There is conjecture that King Solomon may have first seen her toiling in the fields, and she caught his attention and then his heart.

She thought he was a shepherd, and she was attracted to him. Song of Solomon mentions her calling Solomon a shepherd. However, one day the king pulls up in his chariot, and whisks her away forever from the life she once knew! What a great story for those who believe in sappy Rom-coms and other love movies about unlikely matchups!

The lovely maiden had to have embraced her beauty with confidence but not arrogance because she clearly loved herself. Song of Solomon 1:5 (NLT) says, "I am dark but lovely." Many young women today measure themselves by the standards of what society, celebrities, and trends deem as beautiful. Shula loved herself enough not to be concerned with trends or cultural standards of beauty of her time. With all the body shaming and false expectations of what "beauty" is, know that our Lord Jesus Christ loves you just as you are.

Confidence is a great attraction for men. Shulamite was able to stand naked before him unashamed and fully give herself to him. I'm sure that alone was an aphrodisiac for him. Her unabashed ability to look him in his eyes was not something women would do back then, especially looking boldly in the King's face even if he was her husband! Is that one of the reasons she stood out among the others? Is that one of the reasons he loved her so?

Shula is a Hebrew derivative for peace. Just as Solomon also means peace in some translations, it was said that he called her "Shula" - a pet name that is also, as stated, a version of his name. He made it clear she belonged to him.

This reminds me of our Father, who says, "I've called you by name. You're mine. When you are in over your head, I'll be there with you... Because I am God, your personal God, the Holy of Israel, your Savior...That's how much you mean to me! That's how much I love you. I'd sell the whole world to get you back." Isaiah 43:1-4 (MSG) We belong to our Creator God. He is our Father, protector, provider, and more. Never doubt His love for you.

You never know where love will find you. It could be in a vineyard, at Starbucks, in your church, a chance introduction by your Cousin Mordecai, or in the halls of Cooley High, but when Love puts you together, His plans are always good.

"Real love inspires us to never take each other for granted."
~Cynthia D. Jones

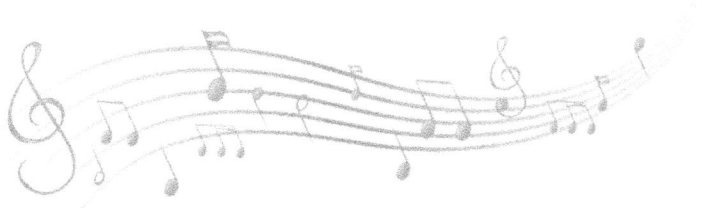

"Music gives soul to the universe, wings to the mind, flight to the imagination and life to everything."
~Anonymous

ENDLESS LOVE
Lionel Ritchie and Diana Ross

"Let love and faithfulness never leave you . . .
~Proverbs 3:3 (NIV)

Whenever I read any version of Proverbs chapter 3, my heart fills to overflowing with the intensity and passion. Solomon teaches the importance of love and faithfulness to God and others. The clarion call here is to be obedient to the commands of God, which invites us to remember to love God first and to love His people. All people.

I see a strong message for marriage, almost like a compressed version of traditional wedding vows. Always love, be faithful, show loyalty, and show your spouse an endearing affection that comes deep from within your heart where the Holy Spirit dwells. In your heart, the Fruit of the Spirit—love, joy, peace, patience, kindness, goodness, faithfulness, gentleness, and self-control is nurtured, nourished, and grows.

This passage reminds me of the intensely sensual song "Endless Love," which expresses fidelity, faithfulness, and single-minded focus on a sacred love of two who vow to be together forever. It's a covenant for life, love, and the pursuit of happiness together as a couple. This song is about sharing an honest and deeply fierce love that others can see.

Proverbs 3:3 teaches me that I can truly love my husband the way he deserves through the power of the Holy Spirit living in my heart. The Holy Spirit enables and heightens our ability to express love to one another. It builds the character traits, attitudes, and emotions necessary for a vibrant relationship. It takes all of the Fruit of the Spirit, ALL of the time to pour into marriages—the words, actions, and deeds God wants us to use to bless each other.

When we ask our Lord to fill us with godly wisdom, the Holy Spirit helps us filter and guide our thoughts from negativity and criticism. Godly wisdom leads us to forgive, let go of grudges, and live as I Corinthians 13 teaches us. As we grow in spiritual maturity, we are less likely to dwell on small stuff. God will direct us to the right actions, decisions, and paths to keep our marriage on the road to Endless Love.

I am blessed to have a husband who, while I sometimes complain is not the most romantic, does try. He is a willing student whose loving desire is to please me. We often reminisce about our life and rejoice in our innumerable blessings. Q and I talk, laugh, cry, praise God for His faithfulness over the years, and pray together. During these times I am most assured of our endless love.

"Solomon teaches the importance of love and faithfulness to God and others."
~Cynthia D. Jones

"Never let go of each other, or life will knock you down like dominoes."
~Cynthia D. Jones

FALLING LIKE DOMINOES!
Donaldson Toussaint L'Ouverture Byrd, II

"Two people are better off than one, for they can help each other succeed.
~Ecclesiastes 4:9-10 (NLT)

Have you ever heard a song that stayed with you, and you just could not shake it? I find myself singing it all day in my mind, sometimes out loud as I'm in the car, cooking a meal, or showering. For one whole week, I sang a song that goes back to when I was in college. When they placed that record on the turntable, everyone would get up on the dance floor! Afros were bobbing, fingers were snapping, and everybody was swaying to the rhythmic and smooth sounds of the music.

"Fallin' Like Dominoes" was recorded by Donaldson Toussaint L'Ouverture Byrd, II, who was a jazz, soul, and R&B trumpeter of international proportions. Donald's recordings go back to 1955! He was also a professor at many universities, including the Music Department at Howard University, where he established a group of student musicians to become a fusion group of recording artists with several major hits.

Now that I've given you some background on Donald Byrd and the Blackbyrds, I can move into the message of this devotional. God can speak to us any way He chooses—in His Word, through conversations, in a sermon, in prayer, in meditation, in music, and even in nature. Our responsibility is to be open to hearing from Him and not limit or dictate how He desires to speak to us. The world is not always kind, pleasant, or caring.

Life can be harsh, even brutal at times, but because of His enormous love, our Father wants to communicate, commune, and be in a continuous relationship with His children. If we listen, God may provide a personal message in the words of a song that won't go away. I have heard messages in gospel, jazz, R&B, pop, soul, and some country music that have inspired me to be a better person.

The enemy knows that God connects with us through music, so we must guard our ears with godly discernment to protect our hearts and minds from negative influences. Music has the power to penetrate and alter thoughts, change perceptions about life and create challenges in thinking. It has become a weapon of choice for Satan, mainly used against our young people. Remember, he comes to "steal, kill and destroy" any way he can. Let me clarify that, contrary to popular belief, not all secular music is sinful. You can listen to it, but you must be alert to the dangers in some of the lyrics. Often the words can be deceptively subtle, BUT when a song is inspired by God, it can be helpful. It can reach us at our point of need, encourage us to do better, inspire us to love others, and admonish us to change our attitude. Whether your life is currently hard, or you are experiencing peace and joy God speaks through music.

I love hearing testimonials from couples who have great faith in the Lord and have an unbreakable bond of love. They have conquered trials like dominoes and knocked them all down. I know couples who have battled cancer, brain surgeries, heart disease, accidents, financial problems, and even the loss of a child. They are battle-weary and have physical and emotional scars, but they are holding on to God and each other. These amazing couples give me courage, confidence, and a deeper commitment to my journey with Q.

"Fallin' Like Dominoes" speaks of drawing close to one another, not allowing the enemy to close ranks on you in his attempt to divide and conquer. In trials, the key to facing obstacles is never to let go of each other, or life will knock you down like dominoes.

Trust is a solid foundation to keep your marriage strong. When one leans, prop each other up. Look together in hope and watch God help your problems fall like dominoes.

Music can brighten your day. It can lead you into moments of unspeakable joy. Kick the rugs back, grab your spouse and break into old-school moves to forget about your troubles for a while. That euphoria will remind you that God's got you, and He's the third cord that keeps you firmly connected to Him and each other.

"When a couple stands together and decides to face life hand in hand, life becomes bearable."
~Cynthia D. Jones

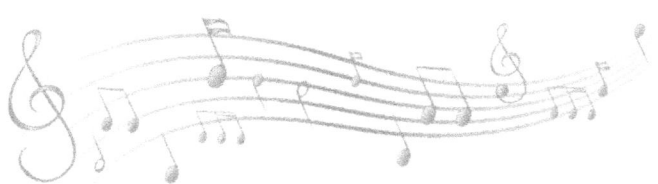

"In marriage, the best teacher and best gift to give your spouse - practice what you've learned from Jesus."
~Cynthia D. Jones

HEAVEN MUST HAVE SENT YOU FROM ABOVE
Marvin Gaye and Tammi Terrell

"Every good and perfect gift is from above, coming down from the Father . . .
~James 1:17 (NIV)

As I watched Q sleep one morning, I reflected on James 1:17. Q was resting peacefully, his breathing was calm, and his expression was relaxed. I realized that my husband is a gift from God. My Father knew in His wisdom that Q was the one I needed to share life and all of its "come what may" situations and journeys with him.

The previous night, he had pushed one of my buttons and I pushed back. But, as we prayed together before bed, we were able to move past our disagreement and rest peacefully. As I looked at him that morning, I could barely remember what our disagreement was about.

Ephesians 4:2 (NLT) tells us to "always be humble and gentle." But, of course, there are times when I know I've been neither humble nor gentle. Neither do I want to admit my complicity in a conflict, especially when my words were not gentle. This passage further challenges us to "be patient with each other, making allowances for each other's faults because of your love."

We remember our love we professed at the altar, and it is our responsibility to treasure it, protect it, and value it. God's love is perfect, and He has placed it in our hearts to love one another as we pass it back and forth between us. We must guard our mutual relationship with the Lord and our marriage above all else.

Marriage Intangibles

First, divorce is not an option; we commit that marriage is for life. Q and I have come close to the line but never crossed it. We wanted to cut those three cords, sever the bond, and run! But praise the Lord; we did not and will not give Satan the victory.

Secondly, we treat each other as we want to be treated. Friday has been date night for decades, with few exceptions. Quality time is valued. Birthdays and holidays are always spent together. We never leave the house without a kiss and without saying, "I love you." The thought that our last words would be less than kind is not a memory we'd want to be left with.

Just a few more intangibles:

1. We strive not to allow the busyness of life to fill our schedules so much that there is no time for each other. One commitment

we make is to sit across from each other to have dinner.
2. Prayer is mandatory in our home. We pray at the top and the close of our day without exception. And throughout our day, we pray for each other. It's a blessing to thank our Lord and Savior, Jesus Christ, as we pray together before we go to bed.
3. In marriage, the best teacher and best gift to give your spouse is to practice what you've learned from Jesus.

A Prayer

Jesus,

You are a kind and caring Lord. You have demonstrated a selfless love, a forgiving love, and a sacrificial love when you exchanged Your life to save ours. You have exemplified a love that sets the standard for all married couples. Let us never forget to bless our spouse with our efforts to love as You love us. We give You gratitude, Father God, for the person You gave us to share our lives with. Draw us closer to You and each other we pray in Jesus' name.

Amen.

Ronald and Carla Huggins were married On August 14, 1999. Their love epitomizes that two are unconquerable when they face life together.

FACE IT ALL
Fred Hammond

"Though one may be overpowered,
two can defend themselves.
A cord of three strands is not easily broken."
~Ecclesiastes 4:11-12 (NIV)

Ok, everybody, this song, no, this entire CD, is my new jam! The words to this song (that I wish I could share) epitomize standing together as a couple no matter what comes our way. Life is not easy. Every day, the enemy throws obstacles and hurdles in our path and shoots arrows at us from every direction. Sometimes he gives full-frontal attacks to destroy Christian marriages. Satan hates marriage and families because he hates God's people.

The words to the traditional marriage vows cover so much of what a couple will face in marriage. However, couples will have to traverse some things they can't prepare for. The Word of God assures us we can make it when we are determined to stand together with each other and with Him.

I stood before God and repeated my wedding vows in front of our friends and family:

I, Cynthia Denise Freeman, take you, Quentin Jones, to be my lawfully wedded husband. To have and to hold from this day forward, for better, for worse, for richer, for poorer, in sickness and in health, to love and to cherish until death do we part.

I had no clue what I was committing to when I spoke those vows! I just wanted to be Mrs. Cynthia Denise Jones. Mrs. Quentin Jones. We loved each other and were committed to being together until death called us home, but the Lord knew we had no idea the journey our lives would take.

I could be like the Apostle Paul in II Corinthians 11:23-27 and list the trials, tragedies, and twists our lives have taken during our marriage. The list is too long to mention them all, but we have had numerous surgeries, including cancer, miscarriages, car accidents, deaths, job loss, and being broke, but not broken. I'm sure you have your own list. Complications, circumstances, critical junctures, crises, and far too many caskets closed too soon. So many experiences could have, or should have taken you out, but for the grace of God and the support of each other.

Satan has many tools to tear at your marriage and destroy your union. He wants to make it easy for you to call it quits and walk away. I have seen many billboards advertising the low costs of divorce. Do not make it easy for the enemy to have the victory of seeing your home divided.

Through reading articles and books, I have learned that there are several reasons for divorce. The main sources of the following information are *Divorcenet.com, Insider.com, the Huffington Post, Forbes,* and the *NCBI*:

1. Lack of commitment
2. Incompatibility
3. Communication—When couples don't talk, don't share true feelings, and find outside sources with whom they communicate.
4. Extramarital affairs
5. Financial problems—irrational/out-of-control spending, keeping secrets, no joint agreement of large purchase decisions, no communication, etc.
6. Addictions
7. Physical, verbal, or emotional abuse.
8. Child-rearing and domestic disagreements
9. In-laws and other external influences,

Other reasons high on the list include illness, religious, cultural and educational differences, and extreme social obligations. Again, Satan's tool bag is massive. It is filled with weapons to wound, divide, break, and tear up your home. The enemy doesn't want marriages to prosper.

Every marriage will face adversity. Some situations will rock the foundation of your home, leaving cracks and disrepair that only the Lord can restore but not every breach has to bring your house down. You will face it all, but together, you can survive.

Pray and do not release your hold on the Lord and each other. Never be too proud to seek Christian counseling as a viable and valuable option. You do not need to feel guilt or shame in admitting you need intervention. Marriage requires spiritual maturity and perseverance. Find accountability partners who will encourage you, stand in the gap for you, and maintain guardrails around your marriage. My words cannot express how important our accountability partners and small group have been in fortifying and stabilizing our home through all kinds of adversity. On the flip side, what a joy it has been to have people who have encouraged and supported us.

Q and I have no shame in witnessing the promises of the Lord that we have lived out in our life. Why? We have experienced God's promises *fulfilled* in our lives. Mark 11:23 (NLT), Jesus says, "I tell you the truth, you can say to this mountain, May you be lifted up and thrown into the sea, and it will happen. But you must believe it will happen and have no doubt in your heart." Mountains of difficulty are removed, difficult relationships end in peace, obstacles have been overcome, diagnoses change, and healing is the outcome. We have waited, prayed, and trusted God standing together as one.

For example, when we were young, Q was a rising star in his office. He was well respected and valued as an employee until a new manager with ideas for his own team decided to lead the business in a different direction. A position Q was being groomed for went to another person, so he quit his job in anger. I know for sure a little pride was mixed in his decision. It took Q almost eight months to get rehired. In the aftermath, we struggled!

Loved ones who understood the job search process prayed for us and slipped us a few bucks when they could. It was humbling and difficult, but we were faithful to manage bills without becoming delinquent. We had to lean on the Word of God to keep us together. There was no denying that God had a plan for our lives, and we had to wait in faith until He answered our prayers for the right job.

One of the greatest lessons Q learned in this particular valley was to continue giving our tithes and offerings. At first, he was angry when he found I was still honoring the Lord with our tithes. He proclaimed we barely had enough to cover our expenses on my check. But, I shared with him, now more than ever, we need to be faithful to the Lord if we want Him to be faithful to us. Q had to remove worldly logic and replace it with the assurance of God's promise to take care of us. When we got on the same page, we saw God sustain us in ways we didn't expect.

May you and your partner find that you are stronger together in the aftermath of storms as Q and I did. Our faith in the Lord and reliance on each other allow us to continually "Walk in Victory!" Keep Christ at the forefront of where you are going and what you are endeavoring to accomplish, and you will get to the other side. Side by side, hand in hand, with the Lord, "Face It All."

"Marriage is designed to grow us into a better example of Jesus' character."
~Cynthia D. Jones

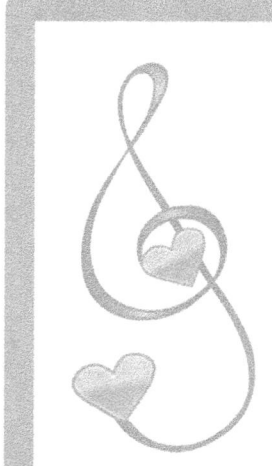

"The blessed assurance is that we are signed, sealed, and delivered by our Father until death do us part!"
~Cynthia D. Jones

SIGNED, SEALED, DELIVERED
Stevie Wonder

*"Therefore what God has joined together,
let no one separate."*
~Mark 10:9 (NIV)

Marriage works best when we follow His plan and design. It's been tested and proven for thousands of years. When we keep Him at the center and follow His Love Book, we will be better equipped to handle the trials all marriages will go through.

It's not easy for two people from different cultures, experiences, ideals, emotions, and thoughts to coexist. Differences and toxic times subconsciously or consciously, are bound to occur. Waking up on the wrong side of the bed is a "REAL" situation. Not that I'm not grateful for each day the Lord gives, but sometimes I just don't sleep well, and I'm a bit irritable. How about you? Did something or someone rub you the wrong way during the day, and do you continue to stew over it when evening comes? Or maybe the kids got on your nerves, and your spouse comes home oblivious to how your day has been and pours last-minute honey-dos on you. The dinner conversation won't be good. That's truth!

Marriage is hard work! Even though we said, "I do," there will be some days when we say, "I won't" or "I don't," and "You can't make me!" Yes, it sounds like a child, but often our behavior is childish when we feel taken advantage of, unappreciated or undervalued. We want what we want and what we feel we deserve.

Q is rarely in a bad mood. That alone some mornings makes me irritable. Why is he always so cheery? I know he lives in the joy of the Lord, and when he says, "I'm walking in victory," he means it 24/7. Sometimes I want to tell Q to be quiet when he's singing show tunes or theme songs from old Westerns early in the morning when I'm still in bed. But then, I have to ask God and Q to forgive me. During those times, Philippians 4:5 (NIV) screams out at me, "Let your gentleness be evident to all. The Lord is near." That verse convicts, haunts, and corrects me...for my good!

Unfortunately, everyone is flawed, and we fall short of God's glory — often. Knowing that as truth, Q and I know we will be on the Potter's Wheel many times throughout our lives. We still strive to be the kind of couple we want other couples to see. We believe in honesty with others to prevent them from seeking an impossible standard. We know we are not perfect, but we were connected by God because He is the glue.

Our God of Love keeps us together. Because we are individuals trying to make our union work, we may understand and interpret situations differently, even if we are both eyewitnesses.

Quick example, Q and I can be watching the same show on TV, and we each have a different opinion or viewpoint of what we saw. Oh, we can have some intense debates over who was the victim and why an incident happened in the story. Why? Because we see life from our perspective and our own experiences behind those opinions. Experiences loaded with feelings and emotions are unique to us as individuals.

As couples, we have to be tuned in to each other's sensitivities and needs. We have to become selfless to help, strengthen, and support our spouses. Like Romans 15:2 says, "Each of us needs to look after the good of the people around us, asking ourselves, "How can I help?" That's exactly what Jesus modeled for humanity.

Marrying Q was the best decision I ever made. Every day has not been sunshine and roses, let alone having one unanimous agreement after another. Conversely, there have been days when I questioned if I was cut out for marriage. It's not for the weak. Together we find strength when we stand on His promises:

- "With God, all things are possible." Matthew 19:26 (NKJV)
- "I can do all things through Christ who strengthens me." Philippians 4:13 (NKJV)
- "Depend on the Lord for strength. Always go to Him for help." I Chronicles 16:11(ERV)

When I look into my husband's eyes and see him smile at me, I have no regrets and only praise God for joining me to this man for all my appointed days on earth.

Here's my dose of wisdom to share with you, "Any time we interface or interact with another person, conflict is possible. How you choose to deal with it affects the quality, love, and longevity of your marriage. We have learned to ask ourselves, "Do you want to be right, or do you want to enjoy peace and harmony by letting some things go?"

Instead, learn to sing together, "Signed, sealed, and delivered, I'm yours!"

CHRIST
MOMENTS OF REFLECTION

- Read Genesis 1:26. What does it mean to be made in His image? What responsibilities did man and woman have?
- Read Genesis 2:18-25. Why did God make a woman for man? How did He make her? What does it mean to be one flesh (or united as one, depending on the translation)? Put a focus on Genesis 2:19. What exactly does that mean to you?
- Read Ephesians 5:21-33. What does mutual submission mean to you? What does respect mean to you? How can you better show that to one another?
- Do you take time to study God's Word and pray individually or as a couple? If not, discuss how you can begin daily Bible study time for your family.
- Do you believe that the Lord had a hand in putting you two together? How so?
- Do you pray for each other regularly? What are the benefits of praying for your spouse daily?

THE MELODY OF MARRIAGE

CONNECTION & INTIMACY

Song of Solomon 3:6-5:1

> *"Come and look, sisters in Jerusalem. Oh sisters,
> of Zion, don't miss this! My King-lover dressed
> and garlanded for his wedding,
> his heart full, bursting with joy!*
> ~Song of Solomon 3:11

In this section, Solomon and Shula have been married in a fabulous wedding with all the bells and whistles. He arrives on the scene in a carriage with its own special sofa for his queen. Her girls decorated this special sofa with purple cushions in a gesture of genuine love for their friend. The carriage is led by sixty warriors in full attire. Solomon is crowned by his mother during this festivity, "his most joyous day."

Before their wedding day, the couple found themselves in hot and intensely passionate situations when Solomon was doing his best to take temptation all the way for a home run! Shula was ready, but she stopped herself, at least in this particular situation. Later she uses that experience to teach her young friends. "Don't excite love, don't stir it up until the time is ripe and you're ready" Song of Solomon 2:7 (MSG). Shula was giving them advice from her personal experiences, "Don't start something you are not mature enough to handle."

Now that they were married, nothing was stopping their release of stored-up passion and love for each other. They are ready to celebrate with ecstasy and passionate love as God intended marriage to be. It's time! In chapter 4 of Song of Solomon, they consummate their marriage, taking their time to enjoy each other head to toe…all night! Solomon would have loved the commercial-free music stations we have today.

Shula and Solomon showed no inhibition, shame, or withholding of giving themselves to each other fully, completely, and confidently. God's desire for His children is that we find everlasting satisfaction in the arms of our spouse. Love can remain enjoyable and strong as we learn to love each other selflessly and without expecting reciprocation. Proverbs 5 says as we mature may we always be captivated by each other's love. The same is true for wives to find satisfaction and rest in the arms of the man she said, "I do" to.

I Corinthians 7:1-5 tells us that our bodies belong to each other as a gift for intimate and ultimate pleasure. We are not to deprive our spouses of sexual intimacy.

As time and life happen, it becomes harder to feel so uninhibited. I'd like to share a comment from a dear friend. We were at dinner one evening with five other couples, and we were talking about how we've managed to remain content in our marriages after "all these years."

Jerome Palmer gave such a sweet and sincere response. His lovely wife, my Sister in Christ, has had some health challenges, but she is one of the most courageous and talented women I know. He said, "The  outer may change, but the inner hasn't changed. Her attitude, personality, loving nature, and who she is to me make her the most beautiful woman in the world!" He further said, "I believe adversity has made us even stronger!"

That was a "drop the mic moment!" Love is a stabilizing force that, when seasoned by time, trials, and testing, should make our union even sweeter. Real love resides in the heart and in the memories of a shared past. When we start to change physically, as we all will, I have two pieces of wisdom for you: 1.) Memorize I Peter 4:8 in the message version and 2.) Buy bedroom lights with dimmer switches! They make everyone look better.

Philippians 2:3-5 (MSG) gives us the keys to building a rock-solid intimate relationship:
1. Find ways to agree with each other
2. Love each other completely and genuinely

3. Be deep-spirited and trustworthy friends
4. Be selfless, seeking other's needs first
5. Don't sweet-talk to get your own way
6. Always value and show respect for your spouse
7. Lend a helping hand

None of these keys begins or requires special physical skills or expertise in sexual gymnastics. Instead, grow in your understanding that mutual respect, commitment, and trust will allow you as a couple to grow, persevere and sustain a vibrant, loving relationship that dually pleases each other and lasts a lifetime.

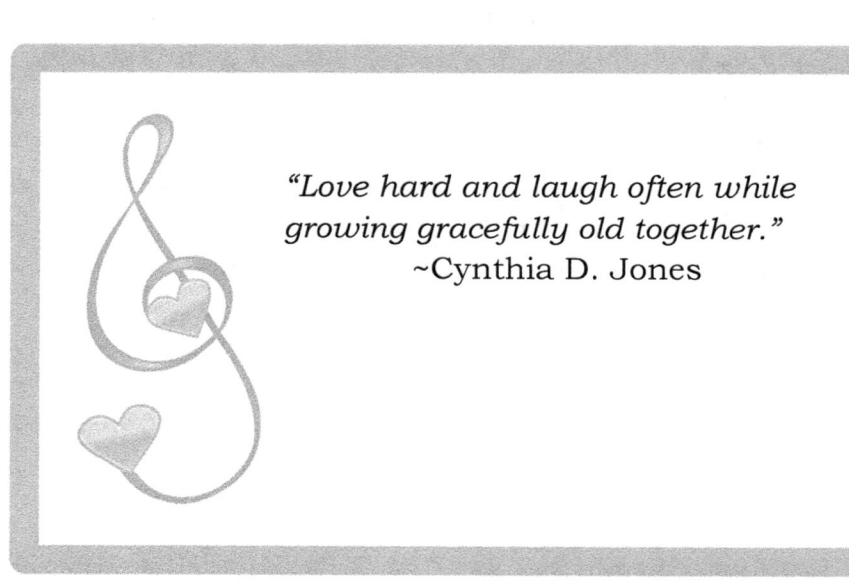

"Love hard and laugh often while growing gracefully old together."
~Cynthia D. Jones

AIN'T NO MOUNTAIN HIGH ENOUGH
Marvin Gaye and Tammi Terrell

"For wherever you go, I will go; And wherever you lodge, I will lodge; Your people shall be my people, And your God, my God.
~Ruth 1:16 (NKJV)

Over the course of our marriage, Q and I moved sixteen times. Almost every move occurred during his thirty-nine years in the automotive industry. Moving so many times was not easy. Before we married, we made many plans, some grandiose, typical of young couples. We wanted a home of our own, a couple of kids who would make us proud, to have some good friends, work hard, party occasionally, travel, and share Christ in a solid church home. We believed we would work 9-5 and come home to each other nightly. Live well, love hard, and laugh often while growing gracefully old together.

I thought I could control the narrative of our future. Fortunately, as I can now say, it did not work out as I envisioned. Q was on the road with his job constantly. Most weeks he left on Mondays and did not return until Friday. I, newly married, had to learn to make it on my own in a new city and initially with no friends.

But one of our dreams became real when we signed contracts to build a house at barely twenty-three years old! So young and green, we realized we needed a refrigerator but forgot we needed a washer and dryer and furniture to fill up the rooms. Somehow we scraped together the funds to make those purchases. There were absolutely no dates or eating out. However, the euphoria of moving into our new home outweighed the fact that we were so broke that a romantic date was climbing into bed, eating ice cream and potato chips, and watching TV.

Throughout Q's employment, we lived in the Midwest, south, east, and west coasts. That included living in Northern and Southern CA, Texas twice, and St Louis twice.

For me, getting any real traction on a career path was difficult because of these moves. After the birth of our beautiful baby boy, and after united prayer, conversations, and mentoring from older couples, we decided that I would stay home to take care of our family. I still served in ministry by volunteering at local charities. I must admit that the absolute hardest part was leaving our friends and church family. And yet, somehow, the Lord has managed to keep many of them in our lives.

We met Mark and Marilyn Townsell at church in St. Louis. We also met Derek and Laurita

Hicks in St. Louis. After several moves for all three families, Q and I moved to Memphis and were blessed to reconnect with the Hicks who also lived there. When we moved to Atlanta in 2004, the Townsell's had already been transferred to the area and welcomed us. These two couples have indeed become family to us. We praise God for the divine intersecting of our lives.

After all those moves, settling down in Atlanta was truly a "God thing." He knew our future forty-four years ago as we made our way from Ohio to Atlanta to celebrate our first anniversary. We drove down south singing Teddy Pendergrass and Stephanie Mills songs all the way. Q and I were so in love, laughing, and teasing as we joyfully promised what would happen when we got to Atlanta and turned those lights off!

Of course, we never knew then where we'd settle when we retired. We never seriously thought about getting older, retiring, or living in a senior community.

Over the years, I have learned about trusting God and remaining faithful to my marriage. I share the following advice with all couples about making big decisions:

1. Pray, and then pray some more.

2. Talk about every decision. Explore how the decision affects each member of your family. Is what's best for one the best for all? It doesn't always have to be one spouse whose career determines where the family lives.
3. Don't let money be the driving force behind a move. Instead, look at all aspects of how every member would be affected.
4. Anticipate God's promise, "And we know that all things work together for good to them that love God, to them who are called according to His purpose." Romans 8:28 (KJV).
5. God is true to His Word, "Commit to the Lord whatever you do, and He will establish your plans." Proverbs 16:3 (NIV).

We are filled with gratitude for the abundance that the Lord has blessed our lives with as He promised, "I have come that they may have life and that they may have it more abundantly" John 10:10 (NKJV). Understanding what abundance means in our mature years is not measured with an expectation of monetary rewards but in different terms.

For us, abundance is the richness of having the love of an ever-expanding solid family, great friends to laugh and share life with, good health, and peace of mind. It's the opportunity to be a blessing in our service and share in God's Kingdom work.

Q is my "Ride or Die," and I am his. And, as we look over our lives, we have no regrets, only gratitude. Whether on the highways traveling and listening to those same songs from the '70s and '80s or chilling on the beach drinking our favorite Virgin Pina Coladas, we sing to each other "Ain't No Mountain High Enough."

To Q, I say unequivocally that nothing and no one can keep me from getting to you. I'm so glad you are my husband; wherever you go, I will follow you, all the way to the moon and back.

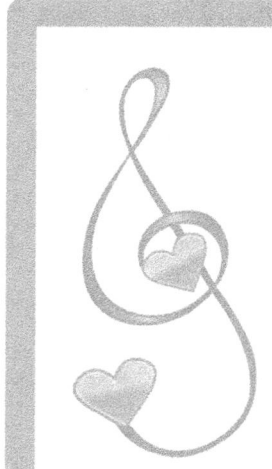

"Marvin Gaye was smooth, but King Solomon was the originator of sweet talk!"
~Cynthia D. Jones

LET'S GET IT ON
Marvin Gaye

*"Kiss me and kiss me again,
for your love is sweeter than wine."*
~Song of Solomon 1:2 (NLT)

During my freshman year in college, my dorm neighbor had a boyfriend. We all knew when he was visiting because for hours on end, they would play "Let's Get It On" by Marvin Gaye. It became a running joke as the girls on the floor passed each other in the hall. We'd say, "We know what's going on in there!"

Over the years, Q and I started making personalized mixed tapes and CDs to heighten our intimate times. We labeled our tapes "Slow Jamz" or "Get You in the Mood" (Whispers) for "Grown Folks Time."

Making those compilations was a kind of foreplay because we talked and laughed as we remembered memories tied to the songs. We'd record them and keep them in the bedroom for our private times.

We never failed to keep "Let's Get It On" in the rotation. That's a classic song that I bet King Solomon and Shula would have had on their playlist. After all, they shared a very active and passionate sex life.

It took me years to get the courage to read through the Song of Solomon. It then took me a few more years to admit that what I read was just what it was, a couple who truly enjoyed being intimate with one another.

It took me so long to understand the Song of Solomon fully because when I was young, a mature saint told me, "Don't take those verses literally. That's God talking to His people, Israel. It's about His love relationship with His treasured loved ones. Those references to kissing and other (ahem) things are not to be taken out of context! Do you think our Father would be explicitly talking about sex in the Bible?"

Now that I know better, I say YES! Isn't He the creator of marriage? He designed marriage and gave married couples the gift of sexual intercourse. If the Bible is both a love letter and teaching manual for all aspects of living, why wouldn't He give us an instructional section on how to enjoy each other as MARRIED couples?

Marvin Gaye was smooth, but King Solomon had to be the originator of smooth talk. I know he had some lines to get Shula ready to get it on. Here is Solomon "rapping" to his lady:

> "Dear, dear friend and lover, you're as beautiful as Tirzah, city of delights. Lovely as Jerusalem, city of dreams, you are the

ravishing beauty of my ecstasy. Your beauty is too much for me — I'm in over my head. I'm not used to this! I can't take it in. Your hair flows and shimmers like a flock of goats in the distance streaming down a hillside in the sound hind. Your smile is generous and full-expressive, strong, and clean. Your veiled cheeks are soft and radiant. There's no one like her on earth, never has been, never will be. She's a woman beyond compare. My dove is perfection...."
~Song of Solomon 6:4-9a (MSG)

Sista Shula showed she could sweet-talk as well as her husband. She was putting it out there to all — he's mine. Don't Play!

"My beloved is radiant and ruddy, outstanding among ten thousand. His head is purest gold his hair is wavy and black as a raven., His eyes like doves by the water streams, washed in milk, mounted like jewels...His lips are like Lillie's dripping with myrrh. His arms are rods of gold set with topaz... This is my beloved; this is my friend, daughters of Jerusalem.
~ Song of Solomon 5:10-16

When Q and I were leaders of the couples class at church, we used to ask volunteers to read passages from the Song of Solomon. You could always tell those who had not previously read the Song of Solomon by the surprised look on their faces. We would see redness on cheeks, voices change, and those "Is this for real" expressions. We would laugh, clearly some "catching the vapors" was spreading across the classroom.

I suggest that you put the kids to bed, throw a blanket on the floor in front of the fireplace, turn on some Slow Jamz, get a beverage, some fruit, maybe some sweet treat, and read Song of Solomon to each other. This will fuel the fire for a low-cost, high-value date.

You're welcome in advance!

"If the Bible is both a love letter and teaching manual for life, all aspects of living, why wouldn't He also give us an instructional section on how to enjoy each other as MARRIED couples?"
~Cynthia D. Jones

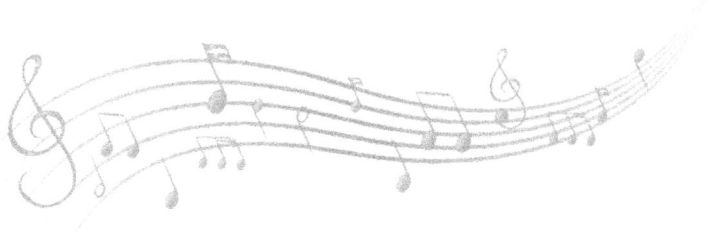

Willie and Theressia Richardson were married for 71 years when he passed on 2/2/23. Their unshakable love for each other stands as a testament for what a God ordained marriage represents.

MY GIRL
The Temptations

"Drink water from your own well — share your love only with your wife. May you always be captivated by her love."
~Proverbs 5:15-19 (NLT)

When I think of the song "My Girl," I am reminded of Proverbs 5. The writer talks about how we are never to take love for granted. True love in a marriage is to be cherished and valued above all other relationships in our lives. Our spouses are to be appreciated and handled with care and respect.

There is no better example of that kind of love represented in my life than the relationship between Willie and Theressia Richardson. We affectionately call the Richardson's "Pops" and "Mom." They will celebrate seventy-two years of marriage on September 16, 2022. I describe them with these adjectives: contentment, peaceful, and devoted. They undeniably show unconditional, sacrificial—FOREVER LOVE. They have a bold yet quiet unapologetic love that has stood the test of time.

Let me share a little about the pure and authentic romance of this amazing couple. One day, Q and I were sitting in the room of Salude

Rehabilitation Center with Pop and Mom. Pop was there recovering from a fall. Q and I agreed that it was one of the most precious and memorable days we have spent with them since COVID-19 began.

    Q and I offered to give their daughter, Marcia, a break. We picked Mom up, took her to breakfast, and delivered her safely to visit her husband. It was sweet to see her dolled up and smelling good. It was thirty degrees outside, so she put on her mink coat and mink hat and had her make-up on so she would look good for her man. Mom appreciated the opportunity to spend time with her beloved husband.

    At breakfast, we talked about their life together. They met, married, raised their children, and lived in Connecticut for decades before retiring in Atlanta. With Pop's fragile health, we talked about their future lifestyle changes. Marcia spoke with them about downsizing. Mom was resistant knowing it would be hard to give up their home with so many fond memories and possessions. Ultimately, she realized that family is most important. We also talked about their love of dancing. I can attest to that because over the years, at different events, they would be on the dance floor cutting a rug!

    We left the restaurant and drove to Salude, the rehabilitation center where he was recovering. When we entered the room, Pops was asleep, eyes closed and mouth open. She quietly but quickly called his name as she kissed him. It was sweet. He immediately woke up and was glad to see her. We arranged the chairs so she could sit next to his bedside and hold his hand.

He said, "I sleep a lot because I feel lonely. I am glad to see you all." Even though his strength is diminished, Pop enjoys the fellowship. Always soft-spoken, his voice was almost a whisper. Pops told us that he bought Mom the mink coat, hat, and a fur jacket decades ago because he enjoyed seeing her look good. Mom checked the label to figure out how old the coat was and said, "There's no way we could afford it now. I am grateful to have it."

They brought his meal, and Mom stopped talking to mention he needed to eat. He said, "I am not hungry," and he continued to talk. "I am grateful for every day God gives me. I realize that my future days are less than my former days, but I am thankful." Pops is a humble man whose wisdom I wanted to glean. I leaned forward in my chair to hear. I did not want to miss a single one of his words.

Pops shared, "This is now my third stroke. I started to go down as it hit me, and Theressia tried to catch me. But I tried to fall soft because I didn't want to hurt her." Tears welled up in my eyes because he has always been her hero, caring for her. Even in his helpless state, he thought first of trying to save his beloved wife and keep her from harm.

We continued to talk for a while about their early days. Mom looked at his hands and saw that his nails needed attention. I handed her an emery board, and she was content to file and lovingly shape his nails. He let her serve him without the need for words.

The conversation shifted to how Mom's sister introduced them. After a short courtship, they knew they wanted to get married immediately. She graduated in June from high school, and by September, they were married. She mentioned more than a few times, "Many young girls back then got married because they were impregnated, but we were in love!" Mom finished with one hand and looked under the cloche to see what he had for lunch. That was a hint. We recognized it was time to leave so he could eat.

Q and I stood to say we were going to have prayer and leave. We joined hands, and I prayed. Pops did not let my hand go. He said he wanted to "say a few words." He thanked the Lord for the privilege of another day, and he thanked the Lord for our visit in a voice so low we could barely hear him. He was tired, and we knew for sure we needed to leave.

I cried in the elevator. Q was feeling emotional as well. When we exited the building, I was overcome with gratitude for God allowing us to know them. They sat on the row behind us at church, and we connected every Sunday for hugs and pleasantries. If my hair was out of place, my hat was crooked, or if something was not quite right with my outfit, she'd always fix it for me. God gave me a "Church Mama and Daddy." I looked forward to seeing them in their sharp, matching outfits each Sunday.

Over the years, Q and I got into the habit of regularly checking on them and I take pictures of them before we leave. Through COVID-19, we continued to do well-check visits, and I'd snap a photo or two. It doesn't matter if he's standing, sitting, or standing with one hand on his walker; he draws the true love of his life near and proudly smiles.

As I think about this passage of being satisfied and content with the wife of your youth, there is no clearer depiction of enduring love than what Pops once shared with me, "It was her smile that caught my attention. Seventy-one years later, she still has a beautiful smile!" Willie, "Pop," Richardson said it then, and he says it today; Theressia Richardson is "My Girl!"

"Honor your spouse by giving the best of your love and trust God to handle the rest!"
~Cynthia D. Jones

THE BEST OF MY LOVE
Emotions

"And let us consider how we may spur one another on toward love and good deeds . . .but encouraging one another-and all the more as you see the Day approaching."
~Hebrews 10:24-25 (NIV)

One morning, during our devotional time and right before an important Zoom meeting with a ministry I serve, Q prayed for me. Once the meeting started, I glanced up and saw him at the door gesturing something, but I didn't know what he was saying. Quite honestly, I was irritated because he knew the meeting was important, and I was trying to concentrate. As the meeting progressed, I heard a ping on my phone and saw it was from him. I peeked and saw this message:

Cynthia:

I love you and thank God for you and your wisdom. I'm so grateful to God for our life together and how He's blessed us abundantly.

I lost all focus at that moment because I was trying not to cry. I exhaled as I was reminded of who I am to the Lord and my man! Oddly, my concentration and contribution to the rest of the meeting were excellent. At this moment, I wanted to say to the Lord, "Thank you for my Boaz! His love makes me want to always give him the best of my love."

I Corinthians 16:14 (NIV) says, "Do everything in love." Few words, but a hard and often heavy command to live out. It's tough to go hard every day with the intent to give your best. In marriage, it can be tough. At the end of a full day, you are spent! There's not much left for anyone, especially your spouse. When you able to finally sit still, you want unencumbered silence. The icing on the cake would be for someone to rub your feet and hand you something to drink!

When two people meet at the altar, they foresee a life with love songs playing as the backdrop of romance and kisses. We can't imagine not being positively responsive to each other's needs. We never anticipate not being available when they need us. Instead, we commit to giving each other the best of our love. But, as life happens, schedules fill up, and commitments cut into what used to be quality time with each other. Priorities change, and the promise to give each other the best of our love leads to compromise or placing our spouse's needs at the bottom of the list.

I always say I can be reenergized to be the wife Q needs because of the Holy Spirit indwelling in me. Two keywords are "intentional" and "priority." When you are intentional in making your spouse a priority on a regular basis, there will be forgiveness, grace, peace, and a rock-solid connection.

Author Stormie Omartian reminds us to pray for our spouses, marriages, and ourselves always. When we do that. God will build up our marriages and lead us into "renewed intimacy and a deeper spiritual union with God." We will be more aware of our spouse's needs as we see each other through the eyes of the Holy Spirit in us. The Holy Spirit will strengthen, encourage and spur us to do likewise for each other. The Fruit of the Spirit is love, joy, peace, patience, kindness, goodness, faithfulness, gentleness, and self-control. With Christ at work in us, there is no taking each other for granted, at least not habitually or consciously. No one is perfect, right? In marriage school is always in session.

This is Mychal and Angela Jackson at their 30th anniversary on July 20, 2015, they have shown many what Phyllis Hyman meant when she said, measure for measure, real love gives us pleasure!

YOU KNOW HOW TO LOVE ME
Phyllis Hyman

"Can two walk together, except they be agreed?"
~Amos 3:3 (KJV)

The lyrics of this song so exemplify what I feel about my husband. This song is truly a reflection of our relationship. Q knows my quirks, pet peeves, and habits. He knows my likes and dislikes, and he knows the buttons that he should not push and the same is true for me. Over time, as we have lived together, we have studied each other through and through.

"*The Master's Degree, Majoring in Your Marriage*" by Fran and P. Bunny Wilson is a "go-to" marriage handbook for me. The book's premise is that a person never graduates from learning how to love their spouse. The writers teach that for as long as we are married, we are in school.

Making your spouse comfortable with what brings satisfaction should be staples like flour and sugar in your cupboard or milk and eggs in your refrigerator. For example, Q knows that I love flowers and traveling. Even though he may fuss about the rising costs of airfare and hotels, he knows that it pleases me more than candy, jewelry, furs, and other niceties.

Likewise, I know what Q enjoys. If I give him a quiet afternoon to watch sports until his eyes turn square, that's Utopia, especially if I give him a Coke, chips, and wings.

Knowing how to love your spouse isn't always about physical intimacy. We have friends who enjoy road trips across America in recreational vehicles. They visit friends, family, and historical sights. After four hours in the car, I become like a restless child because cross-country road trips are not my thing.

Other couples enjoy sports. I've seen wives take an interest in a sport just to be close to their husbands, only to find they are fans of the team. I know couples who have also developed an affinity for cooking together and some have even gone back to school.

One couple that I admire dearly, Mychal and Angela Jackson, have many common interests as they live their lives to the fullest. They enjoy travel and good music. We have traveled with them to music festivals and concerts and always have a great time.

Mychal and Angela Jackson dancing during the celebration of their 30th anniversary.

What I admire most is that they have taken up "Chicago Step" dancing. Angela saw how much Mychal loved to "Step," and she learned how to do it too. It's so romantic to see them dancing together in sync. At times, I can see steam rising around them!

Showing appreciation for your spouse is providing a cool drink if they are working in the yard, having a Kleenex when sad, preparing a favorite meal, buying tickets to their favorite team or movie, surprising her with her favorite color roses, or ordering him a t-shirt with a slogan, team, or his favorite scripture.

Loving your spouse well is about caring enough to study them to know them better, to grow in understanding of who they are, and show them by working to please them every day.

My point is that the aforementioned couples have found a way to spend quality time that gives them the opportunity to connect, communicate and commit to working on loving each other better.

As Frank and P. Bunny Wilson said, "From sexuality to life goals, you can learn the Master's principles of marriage in His Word." Understand that there will never be a day when you can say I know everything about my spouse. Why? Because we are constantly changing, life is fluid and organic, and we, like life, are always evolving. So put God's plan into action and rediscover the joy of learning about each other to experience the excitement of a growing, vibrant marriage.

With all his fussing, Q is content to be beside me on the beach listening to music and watching the waves. Over the years, we have had storybook vacations to tropical islands, walked the warm, white sands of many Caribbean beaches, had dinners in restaurants along the Champs Elysees in Paris, and watched sunsets over the Mediterranean as we sailed the coasts of Spain. We've been blessed. But some of my most enjoyable and romantic times have been and continue to be spent sleeping in on a lazy day and waking up in Q's arms.

*"It's wise to show interest
in what interests your spouse."*
~Cynthia D. Jones

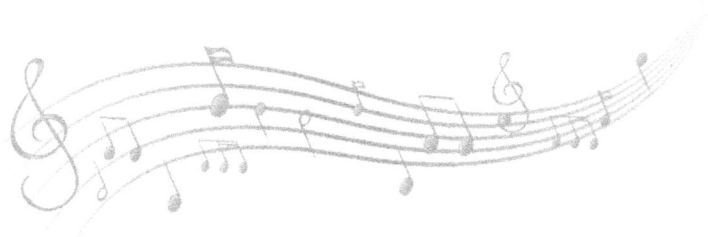

"Genuine intimacy starts early and continues throughout the day."
~Cynthia D. Jones

WHEN I COME HOME TO YOU
Fred Hammond

"Be completely humble and gentle,
be patient, bear with one another in love.
Make every effort to keep the unity of the Spirit
through the bond of peace."
~Ephesians 4:2-3

Because of busyness—demanding careers, personal pursuits, and obligations, husbands and wives can often pass one another like two ships in the night. Therefore, husbands and wives must remember to prioritize time daily to connect. Couples maintain a level of intimacy in the morning, throughout the day, at home, and even when one is away traveling.

Intimacy begins in the morning. It starts with random acts of kindness. Maybe it's not-so-random, more of a daily habit of blessing your spouse with a cup of coffee or tea or rising early together to have a devotional time. There's no better way to enter into the presence of the Lord than to ask Him to keep a hedge of protection over your day in united prayer. That's a shared intimacy that, while not physical, will have a great impact on your marriage.

Intimacy may be initiated as a promise for more when you share a kiss before going out the door. Give your partner compliments, so your voice is the first one they hear, extending encouragement or saying you are attractive to me. Intimacy continues throughout the day when you check-in with your partner and give emotional support or check-in to make sure calendars are synced because you care.

Whoever gets home from work first can start preparing the meal, get the kids started on homework, or set the atmosphere for a calm evening to unwind together. You can watch a movie, talk, go for a walk, or run a relaxing bath for one or two. That is how intimacy continues before you get to your bedroom.

An intimacy killer: One of the things I learned as a young wife from one of my spiritual mentors is not to give your spouse a water hose of information as they walk through the door. Let them get in the door, decompress a moment, relax, and then gently speak about concerns, maybe over dinner or when you are alone.

> *"Do not give your spouse a water hose of information as they walk through the door."*

Another bit of advice is to make sure that your home is a safe haven, a sanctuary of peace where Jesus dwells and that He is glad to be in your home. Pray for the Lord to give you wisdom and courage to set boundaries against negativity and guardrails to keep out anything or anyone who would harm your home. I wanted and still want the peace of God to abound in our home.

Before Q retired it was routine to know each other's schedules. Even today, on Sundays, we sit down and sync our calendars for the upcoming week. When he was traveling, he would call me to see how things were on the home front. I would ask what I could pray for as he finished his day and vice versa. Then, at the end of his day, no matter where he was traveling, he'd call, and we'd pray together before we went to bed. That's spiritual intimacy.

If he was going to be gone all week, sometimes I would put cards in his suitcase, and if I really wanted to surprise him, I'd put a small piece of lingerie in his bag. No message was needed!

One time, I sprayed my perfume in his suitcase one time, and it fragranced all his clothes. He went through the day(s) smelling like me. I can only imagine the thoughts that went through his customers' and co-workers' minds! I wanted to send him the message that I was looking forward to his return home. He needed to know that not only was his wife waiting, but also his friend that he could count on, his prayer partner, friend, and lover.

I had established a signature fragrance that I would wear only for him and only when we were anticipating intimacy. It's been a while, but I would spray it in the bedroom, and it would waft through the other rooms. When he entered the house and smelled that scent, he knew "what time it was." He may be retired now, but I may have to reinstitute that fragrance for times when he comes home late in the afternoon or evening. I want him to always be happy to come home to me.

A Moment of Reflection

Write each other a love letter and mail it. Plan a special evening to open your letters in a romantic setting – maybe with a trail of rose petals leading to the bedroom.

CONNECTION
MOMENTS OF REFLECTION

- Song of Solomon talks graphically about the passionate relationship between Solomon and Shula. Why do you think some people refuse to accept that God put sex in the Bible?
- Do you have a hard time reading some of these verses? Why?
- How often do you and your mate have honest discussions about intimacy? Take time right now to share what you can do to bring mutual enjoyment.
- Do you still date?
- Do you make your spouse feel like they are a priority in your life? If not, discuss what you can do to reignite and refresh your marriage.
- Are you in the habit of saying, "I love you?"
- Do you know your spouse's love language? What do you do to keep your spouse's "Love Tank" filled?

THE MELODY OF MARRIAGE

COMMUNICATION
Song of Solomon 5:2 – 7:9

"(Love) is not self-seeking, it is not easily angered, it keeps no record of wrongs."
~I Corinthians 13:5 (NIV)

King Solomon and his bride had trouble adjusting in the early years of marriage. Their conflict clearly shows three aspects of marriage: connection, communication and commitment. Grace and forgiveness are the best remedies for reconciliation.

Many who read Song of Solomon tend to gloss over this conflict, but in his effort to be totally transparent, King Solomon chose to reveal a not so lovely side of their life for all of our growth and learning.

In Song of Solomon 5:2-6, Solomon returns home REALLY LATE! He knocked on Shula's chamber or bedroom door. In the old days, husbands and wives had separate sleeping chambers. Solomon was tired; he had a long day overseeing his fields, making decisions, and holding court. He wanted his wife's appreciation, support, and affection, but she had locked the doors and her legs!

With all of his wise intellect, Solomon understood her anger, and he didn't use his authority as king to demand she let him in. He communicated his love and tried to woo her on different levels. He said, "Open up to me, my sister, my darling, my dove, my perfect one!" She did not move. He tried to appeal to her compassionate side. He said, "I'm soaked with the dampness of the night, I am shivering, and I am cold."

Shula responded, "I'm in my nightgown, I've got my hair rolled up, and I have washed my feet. I'm not walking across that floor to open the door." He stuck his hand through the small opening in the door and left something with his fragrance on it to let her know he'd been there. It must have worked because when he stopped knocking, she regretted her decision, jumped out of bed, not thinking of clean feet anymore, and began searching the streets looking for him. In her search, she was accosted by the night watchmen who beat and partially disrobed her.

Some theologians say this is a dream sequence woven into the story. I envision the guards as two facets of our subconscious emotions – guilt and shame. They wore her out, but she continued to stay focused on finding Solomon. Friends, when we are overwhelmed by negative emotions it is important to seek our King for forgiveness. Seek Jesus, and when you find Him, present yourself repentant and remorseful.

When she found him, Solomon demonstrated a persevering and committed love when he responded to Shula's refusal to allow him into her room with love instead of righteous anger. He knew in his heart Shula was sorry. He did not throw her wrongdoing in her face, nor did he mention how unappealing she looked after her beating. Instead, he showed grace. He looked at her as Jesus looks at us, lovingly, finding us beautiful in His sight.

Solomon told her how beautiful she was to him. He saw her through eyes of love just as Jesus does when He forgives us. When we confess and seek God's forgiveness, He releases us from guilt and shame, cleanses and heals us, bringing about a reunion of grace that we cannot imagine or deserve. In seeking Solomon, Shula demonstrated repentance.

Scripture says what we say is an overflow from our hearts (Luke 6:45). Our actions, words, and feelings come from what our thoughts have allowed to manifest in our hearts and overspill into tangible behavior, emotions, and words. I was told once, "Don't write a verbal check your behind can't cash!" In other words, don't speak words you will regret. Don't harbor negativity. Our thoughts will determine our feelings, our feelings will determine our speech, and our speech will determine our actions. We must be careful of what or who we allow in our sphere of influence.

Recognize we all fall short of the glory of God. That's why forgiveness is God's solution to our problems. When we surrender our will and pick up His grace, reunion and reconciliation are just a confession away.

Solomon knew that and showed us what grace in action looks like. He forgave Shula and lavished her with compassion, mercy, and forgiveness as he focused not on her actions but his love for her. Jesus does the same for us. I John 1:9 (NIV) says, "If we confess our sins, He is faithful and just and will forgive our sins and purify us from all unrighteousness." Forgiveness allowed him only to see his wife's beauty.

"Pride is only interested in who is right in a marital disagreement. Humility is interested in what is right for the marriage relationship."
~Quentin Jones

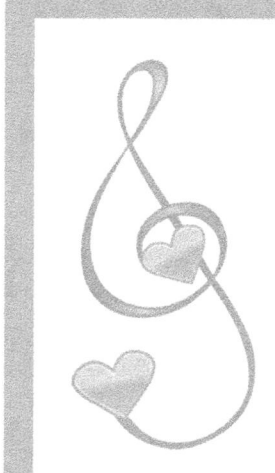
"Forgiveness opens the heart for more capacity to love."
~Cynthia D. Jones

WHAT'S GOING ON?
Marvin Gaye

My dear brothers and sisters, take note of this: Everyone should be quick to listen, slow to speak, and slow to become angry."
~James 1:19 (NLT)

Our Father cares about every broken place in us. Brokenness leads to distrust, anger, bitterness, unforgiveness, or any negative emotion we experience when we've been hurt. He wants to heal our wounds, replace our tears with joy and give us a praising heart instead of gloom. Even when we don't know how to move forward and begin to rebuild trust again, even when we can barely look at each other without pain and anger, we can trust God to be our reconciler and heal our wounds.

Matthew 17:20 says all we need is mustard seed-sized faith to see God work miracles in our lives. So how much do you believe that God can repair your marriage? How much do you really want Him to? For those who have mountain-moving—even mustard seed faith, God wants to show up and show out!

I have experienced mountain-moving moments in my life and in my marriage that have blown my mind! In our mentoring of other couples, Q and I have seen couples in severely bad shape, hostile, and on the verge of divorce, but they ultimately sought the Lord and were blessed with miraculous healing!

Lydia and Malcolm were one of our most challenging couples. They kept us on our knees. When they came to us, she had already kicked him out of their home. We shared scripture and asked them to read those scriptures together, but they did not do it. We asked them to pray for each other, but the wife was so angry that she was unwilling to pray for him and certainly did not want him praying for her! We suggested books, and all she could think about was keeping him out of the house. Reading together was out of the question!

Q and I prayed about how we could reach them and asked God what He wanted us to do for them. He showed us that what she needed was someone to listen. Someone she could confide in as she laid all their dirty laundry, mostly his, out in the open. Lydia wanted a safe place to vent, someone she trusted. Someone she knew would still love her and let her be as angry as she needed to be. Because we loved them both, Q and I were more than willing to be the recipients of this steaming, boiling casserole of bitterness.

Malcolm knew he still loved her and wanted the marriage to be reconciled, so he agreed to sit and listen even as he grimaced and twisted in his seat as his dirty dark secrets were revealed. When Lydia exhausted herself and was empty, we asked Malcolm to respond. All he could say was, "I'm guilty." He admitted to each grievance Lydia spewed out. He was remorseful, repentant, contrite, guilt-ridden, and ashamed. We could almost slice the tension in the air that emitted from them both. At that point, Q and I knew our words would not penetrate. So we invited them to go off to another room to talk and pray. Reluctantly, they agreed.

For a while, we heard loud talking, but we could not determine what was being said. So we decided as long as there was no cussing, banging, or thuds, we'd leave them alone. After hour one went by, we assumed they must have been interacting. Probably more Lydia than Malcolm, but he had strong shoulders fortified by his love for her. He was willing to endure her purging if she forgave him.

After hour two, the yelling had stopped and we could distinguish two voices. Q and I were praying during this unplanned tête-a-tête. After four hours, they emerged. We could tell there had been tears, sweating, and other signs of intense emotions. They sat down, and Q said before you speak, let's pray. I don't remember the prayer, but the scripture that comes to mind now is Psalms 19:14 (NLT). "May the words of my mouth and the meditation of my heart be pleasing to You, O Lord, my rock and my Redeemer."

The first thing we noticed when they came through the door into the room was that Malcolm allowed Lydia to come in first. She didn't show any rejection of his gesture of courtesy. He thanked us for taking the time to allow them to come over. He then apologized and said they had no intention of taking up our afternoon for so long. We expressed that it was important to us at that moment to serve them and help them to get to a better place.

Malcolm said that although many things were uncertain, at least he fully understood her pain and how his actions deeply hurt his wife. I asked Lydia how she felt. Besides being exhausted, drained emotionally and physically, she felt that she had been able to get everything off her chest for the first time in six months. She was embarrassed for showing such a high degree of emotion and told us that her words and actions were not characteristic of who she was. Because we knew them and knew her usual genuinely sweet spirit, we said no apology was necessary. We assured her that we were okay. Since it was so late in the day, we concluded the session. It had been six hours, but there was some progress. Malcolm was still not invited into their home, but they both agreed they'd like to set up another time to meet, and we gave them homework.

We met with them a few more times. Praise God, they eventually were able to pray together. Both of them realized that they contributed to their marital woes. Soon there was forgiveness on both sides. They resolved not to repeat their offenses. Malcolm's restitution was that he would have to work to rebuild Lydia's trust. She would agree not to bludgeon, abuse, or punish him for the hurt he caused her. She also decided to let him move back in. It took time, constant communication, check-ins when he was away, honesty about their feelings, and a commitment to prayer and periodic check-ins with us.

This marriage is thriving and healed. Proverbs 17:9(NLT) "Love prospers when a fault is forgiven." One would never believe this marriage ever had desperately serious problems. Forgiveness is the bridge that brought these two back together. United prayer, learning, and holding to God's promises in His Word are the guardrails that kept them from dismantling their marriage.

This is how we labeled the sessions:

1. "What" – What is the problem? What caused the tension? What's going on?
2. "Why" – Why is there a problem? Why are you not able to connect?
3. "How" – How did the problem escalate to this level? How do you get to ground zero again? How do we get to resolution and healing?
4. "When" – When the enemy rears his ugly head, how will you fight him?

Love prospers when a fault is forgiven.
~Proverbs 17:9

"In disagreements, one of the keys to healing is to learn the difference between hearing and listening then get tuned in to your spouse."
~Cynthia D. Jones

CAN WE TALK?
Tevin Campbell

"Bear with each other and forgive one another if any of you has a grievance against someone. forgive as the Lord forgave you.
~Colossians 3:13 (NIV)

When talking with your partner, try to look at each other to listen actively. There is a difference between hearing and listening. When you divide your attention, fail to watch facial expressions, or pay attention to body language, you can miss critical nonverbal cues that your partner is trying to share. For example, your brain may compute what is being said, but there is no real thought or intake behind the conversation.

When Q divides his attention between fully listening to me and doing something else, I get a little salty. I'll say, "Did you really hear me? Were you listening? Can you just look me in my face and give me your undivided attention so I can talk to you?"

The O'Jays sang a great song about communication after an argument called "Last Night." I think this song teaches that we need to weigh our needs against our partner's needs and be present in the moment when we talk to them. Discern when the best time is to have a conversation with limited distractions. For Eddie LeVert and his lady, it seems their dispute had gone well into the night. In the early morning hours, they talked, listened to each other, they even cried, and the result was a passionate reconciliation. They recognized they weren't ready to give up and they prioritized their relationship when they took the time and energy required to get them back on track.

In disagreements, the key that keeps the doors open to each other is never to stop communicating. If the tone and temper escalate, it may be necessary to break away to calm, pray, and let the steam leave the room. But don't allow too much time to pass, and definitely plan to come back together to resume the conversation. You must both have the attitude of Christ, which is to "speak the truth in love" and know that forgiveness is two-sided, and peaceful resolution is the goal. Ephesians 4:15 (NLT)

When you get into an argument, can you allow the love of Jesus that resides in your soul to take control? Can you let the Holy Spirit landscape your heart by uprooting the bitter roots, guilt, and shame that have grown and manifested their way into dominance? Will you allow the Holy Spirit to fertilize, replant and tenderly nurture and groom your garden with the Fruit of the Spirit again?

Almost everyone has heard Psalm 23. Almost everyone can recite at least the first verse. But have you applied it to your life? Have you considered applying it to all that is important to you? How about your family? How about your marriage when times are harsh?

"Lord, You are my Shepherd; I shall not want. He maketh me to lie down in green pastures. He restoreth my soul" Psalm 23 (KJV).
We all need a time-out. We all need a period/moment in our individual lives and in our relationships where we need to consult with our Father — taking our concerns to the One who is always available. The One who is waiting for our recognition is our Shepherd who cares. Slowly ponder those words, or as Q says, marinate on "the Lord is my Shepherd, I shall not want."

Our Shepherd cares for, watches over, understands the habits, and is prepared to protect, provide for, and risk self to ensure His sheep are safe. Our Lord does all of that and more because he knows, anticipates, and is supernaturally equipped to ensure we have all we need. We shall not want with Him.

It's invaluable for us to know that and to take the liberty to seek God individually and as a couple, especially when there is discord. Sometimes we may not want to discuss our marriage with another person because of privacy, pride, or because the pain is so great. Please remember, we don't have to do life alone. We don't have to suffer needlessly in our lives and marriage. Jesus says, "Come unto Me, all you who are weary and burdened, and I will give you rest." Matthew 11:28 (NIV). Rest in His pastures. Sometimes a change of scenery or a change of pace can give you the change you need to refresh your marriage.

Solomon and Shula knew that.

When things got hectic for, and between them, they were wise enough to take breaks, time-outs, and get away. They went to the country, to David's pastures (Solomon's father), they went to beautiful gardens, and to a country inn to refuel, refresh, and renew themselves and their love for each other. They spent time reconnecting, talking to work out and on their differences, decisions, and disagreements (Song of Solomon 7:10-12).

We need to do this with Jesus as the intercessor, our Father as the Overseer, and the Holy Spirit as the director. Go with your spouse to a peaceful place, get some rest, pray together and then make decisions on one accord. Stop and smell the roses as a couple. That means take the time to appreciate what's good in your life and enjoy it. With clear minds, rested bodies, and calm spirits, much will be accomplished. Get the foxes out of your garden, the wolves of sabotage and destruction who come to steal, kill, and destroy your marriages.

God promises we shall not want when we come to lie down and give our grievances and angry emotions to Him. He restores our souls, heals what's broken, mends and repairs. We must trust Him to be the mediator and trust the Word to be a source of wisdom, truth, and authority of guidance.

Maintain open minds, open hearts and open spirits that are willing to touch and agree. Communicate, talk it out. Seek a counselor if you need professional help/intervention. Know for sure that our Lord and Savior, our Shepherd holds open reservations for you in His pastures. Come humbly to Him in faith. He is our Great Shepherd and Reconciler of peace.

*"Go to the source
to get information,
don't entertain rumors!"*
~Cynthia D. Jones

I HEARD IT THROUGH THE GRAPEVINE
Marvin Gaye

"A troublemaker plants seeds of strife; gossip separates the best of friends."
~Proverbs 16:28 (NLT)

Beware!

When you are married, you have to protect your heart and mind from people speaking things into your soul. Sometimes, negative words and curses can enter in by what and who you listen to. So don't let what you hear simmer in your spirit. Entertaining the wrong opinions can lead to outsiders feeling entitled to render opinions, judgment, and pronounce verdicts on your marriage. It is not okay for everyone to be in your business!

Forget about naysayers who criticize your marriage. Listen to God and do what He tells you about your marriage! He'll give you the courage to leap over and move ahead with your head up as you fight for your marriage and family.

Stop running other people's races. When I married my husband, we became a team, and the only one in charge of **Team Jones** was Jesus. Others will try to tell you how to live your life, their way. They will set up detours and obstacles and try to steer you to dead ends—if you move off the path God has established for you. On the road, there are warning signs, traffic control signs, and cones to tell you what to do for your protection. We go to traffic school and take courses to learn how to be safe out on the highways and streets. Our Father has given us similar guidance. His Word was written for our protection, wisdom, growth, and survival. Proverbs 3:5-6 lets us know that the Holy Spirit is reliable and trustworthy to carry us along our paths in life.

People, many of them well-meaning, will sign you up and put your name on their lists and give you assignments without even asking you! They will get in your business and try to get you disqualified from your team so you can do their bidding. They will try to invite themselves over to your home, get in your space or jump in your car and say, "I'm going too."

Over the years, I have had to filter bad advice from meddlers. I have had people with the unmitigated gall tell me, "Oh yeah, I know you decided to do this, but my way is better." Dear friends, run your race for Jesus with unwavering faith, effort, and endurance. I made the mistake of wrongly respecting people's opinions that I thought had good sense.

Here is a list of a few foolish things people have told me:. These are cliches, myths, and urban legends. Beware, what we consider common sense/knowledge is not always God's truth for marriage:

- All men cheat. If he's a good man, live with his infidelity.
- Accept bad behavior if he's a good provider.
- You can do bad all by yourself.
- He's not a man if he earns less than his wife."
- Keep nagging, and you'll break him down to get what you want.
- It's ok to have a pair and a spare.
- Buy it and hide it in the car. He won't know.
- You work hard, and you can buy and do whatever you want.
- You don't have to tell your spouse everything.
- What's mine is mine. What's theirs is mine.
- Keep a separate account for rainy days.
- Keep a bag packed cause you never know.
- Your kids come before your husband/wife.
- "I can always get another spouse, but I will always have my friends."
- He ain't your daddy!. She ain't your mama!
- "Girl, it's ten women for every Black man. You get him; you better keep him happy."
- It's cheaper to keep her. Divorce is costly, learn to live with_____

These statements are fallacies from hell! Don't buy into the enemy's lies. Learn how to pray God's Word for wisdom and spiritual filters to discern and defeat the Devil. Be assured, he is coming to attack your home. Speak God's promises over your lives: "No weapon formed against me, or my marriage will prosper. And every tongue that comes against us, You will refute" Isaiah 54:17 (NKJV).

I learned the hard way. Let me tell you one of the cliches that I tried on a boyfriend once. "The worse you treat a man, the more he'll love you." Boy, did I learn my lesson. I was given this advice from someone I should have known better than to trust.

My boyfriend at the time was a really nice guy. He did not deserve the treatment and games I was coached to play on him. It didn't take long before we broke up, and I lost a relationship with someone who cared for and respected me. I found out later that she intentionally meant to break us up.

When Q and I started dating, that advice was repeated to me. I didn't just get the broom, I put it in the trash can and slammed the lid! My Christian values have given me a spiritual maturity and a foundation built on the Word of God. I used the scriptures to "speak the truth in love" to her and left her alone.

Learn to deflect, reject, and protect your home, your marriage, and your peace from negative words by praying for godly wisdom and pleading for the blood of Jesus to cover your family. Satan will use anyone to create hostility and divisiveness in your home. **ANYONE**!

Envy is the mother of gossip.
Discord is the father of divisiveness.

Because people view our marriage as a positive standard, we have had a few snakes who have tried to bring trouble and deceit into our space. So let me assure you if you haven't figured that out yet, one way to get checked real quick is to try to bring discord between my husband and me. We don't have time for nonsense. No lies, rumors, innuendos, gossip, or anything you heard about my husband can survive in our space. Without validation, you will face elimination from our circle. We don't want to hear your Grapevine News!

Unfortunately, a couple of snakes did slither out of the cracks. Vipers mistook our generosity as an opportunity to infiltrate our home with their plots and schemes. They were foolish enough to think they could replace one of us by being a newer model. While foolishness has no expiration date, a fool does!

A strong, faithful, solid marriage takes perseverance and standing on the Word together. As you grow closer to the Lord, you will grow closer to each other. Allow no one to separate you from God's love or each other. It's essential to pray to the Lord for godly wisdom. His wisdom, prayer, and His Word are the best weapons to fight against the enemy's attempt at erecting evil strongholds in your home, in your heart, and in your mind.

*"God's Word is the only true authority
for your marriage."*
~Cynthia D. Jones

"Our former first couple, Barack and Michelle, taught the world what being friends and lovers looks like."
~Cynthia D. Jones

HOW SWEET IT IS TO BE LOVED BY YOU
James Taylor

"He who finds a wife finds what is good and receives favor from the Lord."
~Proverbs 18:22 (NIV)

Social media has been enamored with the relationship between former President Barack Obama and his wife, Michelle. Even as their service in the White House came to an end, people remained deeply interested in the Obamas as a couple. Their story began when President Barack worked for Michelle in Chicago, he wooed her into having ice cream one evening. The rest of the story is the marriage of a power couple totally devoted to one another.

    Barack loves Michelle's intellect and considers her his best friend and confidante. He loves her for being the mother of their two beautiful daughters, Malia and Sasha. Those young ladies have shown themselves to be well-grounded and seem to have handled the spotlight with character, humility, and integrity that is above reproach.

    Former President Obama showed enormous respect for her achievements as First Lady. She instituted many programs and demonstrated a passion for military families, health and fitness for our children, just to mention a few of her many successful projects. Michelle has recently written a New York Times best-selling book, "*Becoming*," which has skyrocketed her brand far into orbit! Everything she does confirms she is a woman of excellence. We all applaud and respect her but never as much as her husband. Her devotion for him is reciprocated. Barack Obama is an exceptional man of accomplishment, our first African-American president with credentials far above reproach. Together they showed the world they are an influentially gifted couple of character, intelligence, and dignity.

    I believe that our former president is grateful that Michelle has been "Ride or Die" with him. He has often said that Michelle never signed up for his journey to the White House but has faced the challenges of being a First Lady with uncompromising courage and strength. Despite her stellar career, she supported, rooted for, and encouraged him. She persisted in giving him wisdom and guidance while being his greatest source of comfort.

    Their love has been a symbol and an incredible example to us all of what God designed marriage to be. So, what can we reap from this amazing couple that we can emulate in our marriages?

1. Our first step is to acknowledge that God created wives to be our husbands' support as their helpmates. Genesis 2:18 (NLT) "It is not good for man to be alone. I will make a helper who is just right for him." Your dedication to your husband will not take away from the essence of who you are and what God has planned for your life despite what the world says. When a man feels empowered and spurred on by his wife, he will be bold in his attempts to slay dragons for his family. Likewise, a woman will be empowered in her career when undergirded by the sails of support from her husband.
2. Pray for each other– always! Even if miles separate you two, know that you can depend on each other to be Intercessors and prayer partners through the aid of technology.
3. Keep it fresh for each other. We never saw them looking haggard and worn down. Michelle always had new and different hairstyles, and both were always well dressed, even when they were casual.
4. Don't let your relationship grow stale and stagnant. Surprise your husband with a new hair-do, a date, and keep your bedroom as a retreat just for the two of you and rekindle the romance.

5. Do everything you can to express your love and respect for each other. Respect makes a man feel appreciated and esteemed. Shaunti Feldhahn says in her book, "*For Women Only*," that she conducted a survey and found men need to be respected by their wives. Ephesians 5:33 commands women to respect their husbands. On the other hand, women need to feel love and security from their husbands.
6. Never let a day go by without telling each other, "I love you." It was so refreshing to see sincere affection, hugging, playfulness, and even kisses shared between our former President Obama and Michelle. I loved their playfulness on the Kiss-Cam at a basketball game. They genuinely love much and laugh joyfully.
7. Let your words be filled with kindness and find contentment in each other.
8. Expect him to treat you like a lady. But we have the responsibility to act like a lady. Allow him to open doors, pay the bill at the restaurant, and hold your hand.
9. We can study Proverbs 12:4 (NIV) and Proverbs 31:10 (NIV). Don't get it twisted. Michelle carries herself with strength and power, but she exudes gentleness and a

sweet spirit when her husband kisses her forehead.

Marriage is an ongoing, lifelong God-ordained assignment. It takes daily maintenance, periodic tune-ups, and quality time to avoid becoming a rusty relic that is useless, unappealing, and without value.

Some great books to read, including "*Becoming*" by Michelle Obama and "*For Women Only*" by Shaunti Feldhahn. Submit your marriage to God and commit to giving your best, sacrificial, unconditional love to each other for the rest of your lives on earth. Every now and then, pretend there's a Kiss-Cam and give each other a smooch in public!

Our spiritual children in Christ, Justin and Sharon Hagan were married October 17, 2015. Without compromise they honestly portray how good it is to be loved.

WHEN SOMEBODY LOVES YOU BACK
Teddy Pendergrass

*"Then make Me truly happy by agreeing
wholeheartedly with each other,
loving one another and working together
with one mind and purpose."*
~Philippians 2:2 (NLT)

King Solomon demonstrated a patient and unwavering love when he responded to Shula's refusal to allow him into her room with love instead of righteous anger.

We see Solomon handle the situation with the wisdom and good sense that the Lord God had given him. When she recognizes her disappointment, maybe agitation/anger, he deals with Shulamite in an extraordinary way. He doesn't even wait for her to apologize for locking him out. Instead, he shows her how glad he is to see her. He brings her back to the bedroom. He adores her with words of affirmation and tenderness. He offers grace and forgiveness without dragging the situation out.

How much better would our relationships be if we could just forgive, show mercy that has been shown us, and love in spite of what transpired. In emulation, we pay forward that we are grateful to be forgiven by Jesus, who died for all of our sins. He forgives us over and over. Should we not also forgive?

There have been times when Q and I were so mad that we did not even want to look at each other. I remember our first year of marriage we had a huge fight. We were living in the Cleveland area. I packed a bag when he left to go to the gym to work off some steam. My plan: "I'm not coming back. I'm gone—at least for tonight."

All day long at work, I was anxious and fighting within myself. After work, I realized I had nowhere to go. We had not been in Cleveland long, and I didn't really know anyone except some members of my new church. No way was I going to let them know what was going on. Detroit was out of the question, especially since it was three hours away.

So what did I do? What could I do? Pride would not let me go home. Pride forgot we didn't have discretionary funds. None! Pride knew I wouldn't go to a dump motel because of fear. Pride decided to take me to the Marriott Hotel near the airport. I swallowed hard when I booked a room.

I thought to myself, *"I'll show him I'm a grown 22-year-old and can do as I please."* But I was too afraid to go up to the room alone, so I wandered to the hotel lobby where they had a Disco. (Y'all remember those?) I slid into a booth and tried to be invisible. Why do old men always radar in on young girls? Soon I had one intruder who I brushed off only to have a younger but still slimy invader. It was dark outside. I was hungry and afraid. No cell phones then. Who would I call anyway? Again no family, no friends, no one close by. I shuddered, thinking about calling someone from our new church. In my mind, I could just hear the criticism, "What is a married woman doing in a hotel by herself?"

So who do you think I called? **I called Q to come and get me.** He did. He trailed me home after canceling the reservation. He didn't admonish me for being foolish. He didn't say it to me then, but he had been worried out of his mind about my safety. We were both so glad to see each other. Glad to be at home together. We talked for hours, apologizing, forgiving, and vowing never to hurt each other again.

My sister-friend, Trudy Fowler, says, "Truth be told" when she is making a serious statement. Here's the truth over the decades we've been together, Q and I have hurt each other many times, but wisdom, experience, and maturity have taught us to show grace and sometimes mercy, just as Jesus has shown us.

Marriage sometimes requires one spouse to carry the load 100% of the time, and on another day, it may be reversed but last for weeks, maybe for the duration of your marriage if there is illness or injury. While the world may accept 50/50, we are called to give 100% to each other doing everything as though "we are working for the Lord rather than for people." Colossians 3:23.

We can only love each other with our best because of the love of Christ in us. Even when I am angry and I can't look at Q, I must look for the connecting bond of the Holy Spirit in him. The Holy Spirit reminds me who Q is, a son of God, my husband, Boaz, and brother in Christ. I see to his heart. Real talk—it still feels good loving somebody (Q), and somebody (Q) loving me back!

Reflective Conversation Starters:

- Talk about a situation, trial, or trauma during the course of your marriage that tested your faith and love for each other and maybe even the Lord? How did you endure? It has been proven that in hard times if a couple learns to depend on each other and the Lord their relationship strengthens. How has your relationship confirmed or disapproved that statement?
- A popular saying in the church is, "We are either in a storm now, just got out of a storm, or a storm is on its way." So how can you learn to hold on and hang on closer to one another to ensure you will survive the storms together that come your way?

COMMUNICATION
MOMENTS OF REFLECTION

- What attracted you to your spouse when you first met? What made you decide, "This is the one I want to spend my life with?"
- How do you handle naysayers, who speak against your marriage?
- How have your differences and similarities contributed to your relationship as a couple?
- How do you connect without feeling you have to trap your spouse in a corner or tie to a chair for in-depth communication?
- Do you have a Christian accountability partner or a couple you can talk to about your marriage?
- If not, is there a small group for couples in your church or community that you can get involved with?

THE MELODY OF MARRIAGE

COMMITMENT

Song of Solomon 7:10-8:14

This is John and Trudy Fowler who were married July 5, 1980. John sums up their marriage this way: "A blind date and a tested faith lead to everlasting love with prevenient grace."

> *"Many waters cannot quench love,
> nor rivers drown it."*
> ~Song of Solomon 8:7 (NLT)

George Elliot said, "What greater thing is there for two human souls, than to feel that they are joined for life – to strengthen each other in all labor, to rest on each other in all sorrow, to minister to each other in all pain, to be one with each other in silent unspeakable memories."

I don't think there is a better way to describe the relationship between Solomon and Shula in the ensuing years of their marriage, after the courtship, the wedding, and the honeymoon. They seem to have an active, yet comfortable rhythm. Their affection remained strong.

In Song of Solomon 7:10 (NIV), Shula, still ever confident, says, "I belong to my beloved, and his desire is for me. It is even more clear in The Message Bible that she is still staking her claim, and this passage is translated to say, "I am my lover's. I'm all he wants. I'm ALL the world to him!" She is not worried about 700 other wives or 300 concubines!

That verse sings of their comfort and security with one another. They have a vibrant marriage and a strong friendship. They share similar interests — being outdoors together in the fields and staying over at countryside inns. I admit I started to giggle imagining this regal, royal king running barefoot through the fields with Shula collecting berries and wildflowers! He found himself laughing and enjoying what made his lover and best friend happy. Solomon found joy in making his wife a "First Place Priority."

There had to have been numerous times when she watched at a close distance how demanding, stressful, and draining his life was. Everyone wanted something from him, wisdom, justice, guidance, money, settling disputes, political favors, and things we can't even imagine. I'm sure she had to take matters into her own hands to protect her man's health and well-being! That's why these getaways were a two-fold solution—time for him to rest and opportunity to spend quality time alone with her.

Chapter eight are the last verses of their love story. She seems to do most of the talking; sharing how wonderful it has been living a life beyond her wildest expectations apart from when she was forced by her brothers to toil in blazing sun working in the fields. She remains infatuated with a shepherd who turned out to be the wisest King in the world. As she ponders, she affirms that nothing and no one, not even the hottest of fires, can quench the thirst for true love. No rivers can drown it out, and no one could ever have enough money to purchase a love that rivaled their relationship. They shared a romance that stood the test of time!

"After our Lord and Savior, Jesus Christ, your spouse is to be priority number ONE in your life, over everything and everyone."
~Cynthia D. Jones

My dear friends Jesse and Angela Walton were married on May 3, 2008. They give us an example of leaning into your partner.

STAY TOGETHER
Ledisi

*Do nothing out of selfish ambition or vain conceit, but in humility consider others better than yourselves. Each of you should look not only to your own interests, but also
to the interests of others.*
~Philippians 2:3-4

I will let my friend Angela tell you in her own words about leaning on your partner:

> The last few months had been tough! We were two months into the first COVID-19 lockdown, and I was suddenly thrust into homeschooling our two young sons. My husband spent his days locked behind the doors of our home office, helping clients wade through the financial crisis that the novel coronavirus had triggered. Uncertainty was high, but the stress of each day seemed even higher as everyone started to adjust to the new restrictions and confinements that COVID-19 introduced into our lives.
> The first weekend of May was our 12th anniversary. We had magically found someone to watch the kids for the

weekend. What would we do with a weekend to ourselves? The possibilities were endless and glorious to imagine!

Over the last few weeks, my husband rediscovered his childhood passion for fishing. He would schedule fishing trips for him and his buddies at a local lake or river, or they would travel to Lake Eufaula in Alabama to go bass fishing. My husband told me that he planned a fishing trip for us on our anniversary weekend. I was immediately offended that he would unilaterally decide to use our anniversary weekend as an opportunity to go fishing!

My face started to feel hot, and I had a negative reaction to the whole idea. My husband started making his case, "It's outdoors, so we will be safe. It's time away from the house together." He said more that I honestly didn't tune in to hear. Because I didn't have any better COVID-19 compliant ideas, I reluctantly relented.

After weeks of hearing fishing tales from my husband and his friends, I was determined I wouldn't be going home empty-handed. I would represent and catch me a bass! I wore all pink for women everywhere, symbolizing that I could do this with feminine style!

Our drive to Alabama was peaceful. We had a chance to talk and listen to music. When we arrived and got on the boat, it was a perfectly picturesque day! The bright sun shined, cascading shimmering light on the water. The warm weather was met with a tranquil cool breeze that made the lake gently glide as it formed a subtle current. I took a deep breath and soaked in the moment. Nature was singing a sweet song, and I finally exhaled to release the tension of the last few months.

My husband had caught several fish, and I was starting to get discouraged. I was focused and intent on proving to myself and others that I could do this. I had been watching the fisher guide, and my husband and I copied their techniques. I studied how they held their rods, how they cast, and especially how they kept no slack in their lines. Then, all of a sudden, it happened. I had something on the hook! I reeled and reeled, all by myself. They netted the fish, and wouldn't you know that I caught a five-pound bass.

That was the only fish I caught that day, but it was the largest catch of the day! We took pictures at the end of our trip to capture the results of our fishing expedition. There I was, with my head held high and chest stuck out proudly next to my husband, enjoying our day out on the lake with my prize catch!

As we drove home, I told my husband I had a wonderful time! He had shared his love of fishing with me, and I received a wonderful gift from him. Although I didn't know it, the serene time in nature with my husband was exactly what I needed. We spent quality time together laughing, talking, fishing, and loving on each other. We used the rest of the weekend to celebrate our anniversary in other ways.

I learned a valuable lesson – it's sometimes good to yield and lean into your partner's interests and hobbies. You might learn something new, and you might enjoy the journey!

"It's sometimes good to yield and lean into your partner's interests and hobbies. You might learn something new, and you might enjoy the journey along the way!"
~Angela Walton

"Faith builds a home and prayer fortifies it."
~Cynthia D. Jones

A HOUSE IS NOT A HOME
Luther Vandross

"As for me and my house, we will serve the Lord."
~Joshua 24:15 (KJV)

When Q and I got married, we determined we would be a house that served the Lord.

To help us we have surrounded ourselves with Christian couples who are committed to having a marriage that pleases God. Couples who are loving, caring, and devoted to each other. We need friends who understand the importance of holding each other accountable to raise families that serve the Lord.

You can't fix what's going on inside with what's outside your house if God didn't contract them for you. I would never listen to or even consider hiring a contractor who did not have experience repairing, building, or doing any work on my home. My home is too valuable to my family. Can you imagine paying thousands of dollars to an inexperienced builder/contractor only to be sitting in your home and the first rain comes, and you have leakages and rain pouring in from your roof? That contractor was ill-equipped to handle the repairs seen and unforeseen on your property. As a result, you suffered loss, more damage, and wasted time.

For me, too many subpar contractors are trying to tell us what to do about our marriages. Books, seminars, workshops, and retreats promise they have the answer to a better marriage. Some of these so-called experts have never read the Bible and can't tell you a single verse. How many of us have friends or family members who claim to know what is best for our life? They may mean well, but they really don't believe in marriage, they don't believe that marriage can last, or to them, fidelity is an unrealistic myth.

I can't tell you the number of times I've had couples come to us when their marriages were in jeopardy because they listened to advice from someone who was not trained or experienced to help fix the problem. It is mind-blowing that a married person would listen to someone who's never been married. There are celebrities, who have never been married, and yet call themselves experts in marriage. Wisdom tells us to beware of fools who talk long and talk wrong. Avoid those who like to hear themselves pontificate. Proverbs 18:2 (NIV) says, "Fools find no pleasure in understanding, but delight in airing their own options."

To fortify my home, my family, and my marriage in the early years, we set some unwritten but agreed-upon standards. We would go to church regularly. Whenever we moved to a new area, one of our firsts after finding a good neighborhood, a good home, and a good school for Justin was finding a good church home, that was essential.

It's important who and what you invite into your home. First, establish a pattern of praise and worship in your home. Speak prophecy over your spouse, family, yourself, and home. When things are good, praise can be forgotten when the heat is on: someone is ill, troubles are brewing in your marriage, or in the midst of financial concerns. God hears from you day and night until the storm passes. Let Him get familiar with your voice in good times.

When Justin was around two, we established a daily family devotional time by using a children's Bible. We read stories to him, sang songs he could remember, and prayed together. Of course, he didn't understand everything, but it was important to begin a routine of teaching him who our Father is. We wanted to teach him how to maintain a relationship with the Lord, and to worship Him for who He is to us as individuals and as a family.

As he grew older, Justin would read Bible stories to us. We continued this until he went away to college. For us, a house is not a home without our Lord and Savior knowing He is welcome.

One of my favorite shows is *"Fixer Upper,"* with hosts Chip and Joanna Gaines. One of the things Chip looks forward to on every episode is Demolition Day. Tearing things down and breaking down walls and doors with his sledgehammer is exciting to him. As I'm writing this particular chapter, I'm thinking of how that is a metaphor for the world. (No shade to Chip.)

If a marriage isn't working in its current state, the advice from subpar marriage contractors or maybe marriage distractors is to tear it down, get rid of it, and build something new. But is that our Lord's way? Is it even what you as a couple want to do? You may have years of investing all you have, all you are in your marriage. Blood, sweat, tears, prayers, energy, emotions, financial sacrifices, and let's not forget the children born into your relationship. Beware of those who say too easily- it's over, get out, walk away. When a man sees destruction, God may say, it's worth the time and patience for reconstruction. Remember, we are all a work in progress.

Again, surrounding our lives with like-minded friends, family, and church family helps to fortify the walls of our home. These people help us build ramparts and create firewalls and barriers against the enemy's attacks. We all need folks to help strengthen the foundation of our home through prayer, encouragement, support, and even to stand in the gap with being a village to help us raise our children. Over the years, men like Mark Townsell, Derek Hicks, John Fowler, and Jesse Walton have poured godly wisdom into Justin. We were glad for their support during the times when J preferred hearing a different opinion than ours.

I'm not ashamed to say that it took this long, but I've learned not to measure my life, marriage, or family by the world's standards. With the influence of social media, I've learned that everything that looks real is not gold. Everybody has some struggles, imperfections, discord, unruly kids, some in-laws who are out-laws—some stuff that ain't perfect in their homes. So pray for them and yourself to draw closer to the Lord and find help in Him. (I hope I wasn't too cynical, just expressing the truth). Many of us tend to focus too much on what's going on in others' homes and lives and forget to focus on our own homes. When a home is neglected, it crumbles.

Let the peace of God rule your hearts, souls, and minds then we will enjoy His peace.

"Marriage: Love is the reason. Lifelong friendship is the gift. Kindness is the cause. Til death do us part is the length."
~Fawn Weaver

"Solomon and Shula's tested marriage reveals to us that true love can never be bought or compromised by happenings, infiltrators, intrusions, or invaders."
~Cynthia D. Jones

NEVER TOO MUCH
Luther Vandross

"And now these three remain faith, hope, and love. But the greatest of these is love."
~I Corinthians 13:13

Now you know I couldn't write a book on the melody of marriage without including one of our all-time favorite singers. The real problem was to decide which Luther Vandross song to select because there are so many: "Don't You Know That," "So Amazing," "Love Won't let me Wait," we love "Here and Now," and who can forget the classic, "If This World Were Mine" with Cheryl Lynn.

    I chose "Never Too Much" because once Luther went solo, this was the first song I remember hearing. This song went straight to the top of our playlist whenever we wanted to dance! To this day, we try to outdo each other by singing the verses with the least mistakes! I take a stanza, and Q takes the next, and we duet with Luther as he sings to his loved one about his commitment. Luther sang that there are never enough days, nights, kisses, or times when he held her that could satisfy him.

    In our early dating years, Q and I planned each day with the intent to see each other. We would talk for hours on the phone. There were times I'd go to sleep with Q still talking to me. He'd be met by silence or the sound of my breathing because I'd fallen asleep. I was totally at peace to let his voice be the last voice I heard each night.

As we move to a close in the final chapters of Song of Solomon, the couple is evidently still enamored with each other. Now it appears their love is even stronger and more passionate than ever. Shula confidently says in Song of Solomon 7:10, "I am my lovers and he claims me as his own. In Song of Solomon 8:6-7 she declares, "(Love) burns like a mighty flame...many rivers cannot quench love."

Solomon wrote in Song of Solomon 4:9-10, "You have captured my heart, my treasure, my bride. You hold it hostage with one glance of your eyes with a single jewel of your necklace. Your love delights me, my treasure, my bride."

Solomon and Shula's tested marriage reveals to us that true love can never be bought or compromised by happenings, infiltrators, intrusions, or invaders."

No one and nothing can destroy the kind of love Shula wrote about when she said, "Your love is better than wine" back at the beginning of chapter one.

Even as we get on each other's nerves and as time has slowed us down a bit, Q and I remain committed to the Lord and to each other. I still treasure his kisses and hugs and we, like the King and Shula, enjoy quality time together - be it quiet dinners, laughing with our friends, or just the satisfaction of looking across the room and knowing we are near and still dear to each other.

A Prayer

Dear Lord,

I make our marriage an offering to You, Lord. I lay us at Your feet. I know You accept only pure, unblemished offerings but take us as we are, Lord Jesus. Cleanse us from all unrighteousness and work to fix us from the inside out. We confess that we have not walked in Your will. We confess we have been selfish, self-centered, unkind, and thoughtless towards each other. Our words have not always been gentle as you instructed us in Philippians 4:5.

It saddens me that You have seen when I have been ugly to my spouse or others with my words. We pray for the Holy Spirit to set a guard over our lips and set a guard over our hearts. Mow away the weeds of discontent, anger, bitterness, and unforgiveness. Help us to be more like you. Let our words and actions towards each other be pleasing to You. We thank you, and may we always remember how fortunate we are to have each other.

Amen

Strive to keep Christ in the center of your marriage. Maxwell describes being grateful for finding the love of his life.

FORTUNATE
Maxwell

"Who is this I see coming from the country, arm and arm with her lover?"
~Song of Solomon 8:5 (MSG)

Solomon and Shula are returning from their countryside getaway. The chorus of their friends and townspeople notice them coming back to town.

People are always watching to see what you are doing. The motives are different but make no mistake; people want to know what you are doing and how you're doing it! Solomon and Shula gave them something to talk about. Two lovers who were also great friends — holding on to each other as they walked along, seemingly oblivious to everyone but each other. Quality couple time alone is mandatory for the growth and durability of your marriage. It helps to keep the fire burning hot in your marriage.

I admire Shula's astuteness in seeing the importance of spending quality time alone and away from the daily grind of life. As one flesh, we are called to take notice of our spouse and to show a vested interest in their personal health. We are accountable for making sure we both eat right, exercise, rest and get preventative care by regularly going to the doctors. Respites and vacations to unplug are also necessary. Vacations don't have to be costly. There are getaways for every budget. Don't, discount the value of a respite as important to the health of your marriage.

Pre-retirement, Q had great demands on him as well (of course, not to Solomon's extreme). Someone was always seeking his time, energy, presence, knowledge, expertise, and mediation for one situation or another. He was constantly on planes. At times I had to write myself into his calendar and take him away.

Now that he is retired, Q remains extremely active in ministry, serves on boards, is in school, and was recently recertified as a minister. All great, but I have to be his helpmate first and see when he needs to unplug. Just recently, I had to make plans to get him out of town. Now I can't imagine Q picking berries and frolicking barefoot in anybody's fields. Still, I'm not opposed to using my feminine wiles like Shula to get him to rest, relax and enjoy reconnecting with me, his wife, and best friend.

In chapter 8, Shula wishes she had been able to have a relationship so close with Solomon that they were brother and sister. At first, it sounded a little creepy, but I get it. Then they could have grown up together, played in the fields as kids, and never missed a moment in time together. I, too, have played that scenario in my mind. What would it have been like to have known Q as a young boy? Maybe then I would understand more about what made him who he is and how his experiences as a child shaped his personality, habits, and beliefs.

One thing for sure is that Q is my best friend. As we continue to see the years pass, we have become closer and more comfortable with living our latter days and enjoying the blessings of the Lord. We don't have to prove anything to each other, and there's no competition to see who's best. We have learned to cheer for each other's victories with joy, without being envious, and to be there to bring comfort when needed.

After almost fifty years, life has changed our bodies and faces. Time is no respecter of persons. But, as my former pastor, Jesse Lee Foster in Dallas, Texas used to say, "that figure eight will become a figure zero at some point so it is important to make sure that you have more than physical infatuation." You need that deep, emotionally connective love that you build through living together, which will fortify your marriage in your latter days. This skinny girl has filled out in places she never expected. But I'm learning to be at peace with my curves and accept that Q loves all of me just as I am.

We don't always have to find something to do outside the home or to be in the company of others to be entertained. We find plenty of laughter and contentment with each other. (I sometimes wish others could see how silly Minister Q can be – but that's my gift to treasure alone.) When we have music playing, and one of our favorite songs comes on, we will stop whatever we are doing and dance until either the song ends or one of us gets tired. I imagine Solomon and Shula having the same satisfaction and joy.

I think of two words to describe their relationship and ours: contentment and dedication. Maybe a third that got us to that place, perseverance. Without God in your marriage, peace is fleeting. Goodness is a strain when you struggle to keep your words, attitudes, and actions kind during the course of your day. Remaining faithful is debatably the hardest when a marriage does not give you what you'd hoped it would be. Pray for guidance.

Marriage is the biggest ministry we as Believers will ever embark on. I'm not saying there will be no bumps in the road, no detours, delays, or harsh weather patterns that create storms, but together you will make it.

Q and I give all glory to God, for He has been faithfully with us at every turn in our marriage.

We have learned to trust Jesus and depend on His Word. Life has been "Outstanding" as the Gap Band sings, and we are "Fortunate" to have found peace and contentment as we continue to sing together.

Make sure to keep these key words in mind as your work on your marriage:

- Friendship—a state of mutual trust and support between two parties/people/entities. A relationship of mutual affection among people enjoying and sharing life and mutual interests
- Contentment—a state of happiness and satisfaction
- Dedication—the quality of being committed to a task or purpose
- Perseverance—persistence in doing something despite difficulty or delay in achieving success

COMMITMENT
MOMENTS OF REFLECTION

- Is your spouse your friend? Why or why not?
- What keeps you committed to your spouse?
- List five character traits that you most love about your spouse?
- Do you agree with Dr. James Dobson, "You don't marry a person you can live with, you marry the person you can't live without?"
- Do you provide true "soul food" to your spouse? Do you keep them strengthened, encouraged, and nourished – spiritually, emotionally, mentally, and physically?
- What did weathering storms with your spouse reveal about your relationship?

CONCLUDING THOUGHTS

"Worship the Lord with gladness. Come before Him with joyful songs. Know that the Lord is God; it is He who made us, and we are His…. For the Lord is good, and His love endures forever!"
~Psalms 100:2-3,5

On June 17, 2017, Q and I celebrated our fortieth wedding anniversary by renewing our vows in front of 110 of our loved ones from all over the country. It was truly a magical evening where we got to visually minister to younger couples by demonstrating that marriage can get better with time.

We danced down the aisle to the altar to repeat our vows to each other. Q sang "I Found Love," by BeBe Winans to me, which, was a surprise. At the reception we all danced to the sounds of Lionel Richie, Jeffrey Osborne, Bruno Mars, Charlie Wilson, Stevie Wonder, Earth Wind & Fire and more. It was truly "A Night to Remember" (as sung by Shalimar).

I'm forever grateful and so in love with my Father, who created me to know him, love Him, and serve Him. But, at just the right time, He gave me tangible evidence of His love by allowing me to live my life with my Boaz, Quentin Jones. I had accepted Jesus Christ as my Savior in 1972, just before I started dating Q.

One day in Sunday School, we sang James Cleveland's, "God Has Smiled on Me." At once, I knew I wanted and needed the Lord to smile on me. I was sixteen and I invited Him into my heart. God changed me and flooded my life with His presence, His grace, and His mercy.

My Prayer for Your Marriage

I pray that your marriage will find a place of contentment that stabilizes your home with a "peace that surpasses all understanding."
I pray for a "stronger than death" dedication that will never surrender to the enemy's attacks. I pray for passion and joy to sustain you through any rivers of turbulence in your lives. I pray that you endeavor to grow closer to God as you decide to get into His Word together in daily Bible study. I pray that prayer is a priority for your family and that you realize you cannot live without it – because you can't!

I pray you all become fruit farmers, praying, growing, and sharing the Fruit of the Spirit with others and making sure to enjoy its fruit as you recognize you are worthy and valued by God. I pray that you find new ways to show love to each other every day, remembering always to keep thanking the Lord for your marriage. Finally, I pray you never stop praising, dancing, and singing together.

    I hope that this book will continue to draw you and your spouse closer. I pray that you have found better ways to reconnect, recommit, laugh, and gain more spiritual insight into God's design for Christian marriages. Christ, Connection, Communication, and Commitment are the tools you need to keep the melody in your marriage.

Cynthia D. Jones

As a Motown Girl, I can't wait to ask our Father about His favorite Motown songs!

ACTIVITIES TO ENHANCE YOUR MELODY

"Success is nothing without someone to share it with."
~Billie D. Williams in the movie *Mahogany*

MUSICAL TIMELINE AND PLAYLIST

On the following pages, create a musical timeline of your relationship; this is the musical backdrop of your lives together. It is just a written history of significant times in your lives set to music. Think of songs in your marriage timeline that have given you joy and laughter, such as the song you first danced to, the song that played at your wedding, or a special song on your honeymoon. Include other songs that may have given you the strength to hold on.

If Solomon had a playlist, I believe that he would have included "Let's Stay Together" in his top five because of Al Green's—"Stronger than Death" commitment to love his woman forever.

With Solomon's God-given songwriting abilities, I know he would have rivaled some of our greats with some of his lyrics: Smokey Robinson, Marvin Gaye, Hal David, Burt Bacharach, Kem, or Maxwell. Not even Al Green or Barry White could compete with his lyrics: Song of Solomon 4:1 (NLT), "You are beautiful, my darling, beautiful beyond words." He said of her, "You have captured my heart, my treasure, my bride. You hold it hostage with one glance of your eyes." Song of Solomon. 4:9 (NLT).

Or Song of Solomon 6:4 -5 "You are beautiful my darling…turn your eyes away from me for they overpower me….(NLT)." Can you believe that she made the King, an experienced lover, blush with shyness?

In Song of Solomon 6:8 (NLT), he wrote, "Even among 60 queens and 80 concubines and countless young women, I would still choose you my dove, my perfect one."
I said he had a lot of experiences, but she is the "ONE" who won his heart, mind, soul, and body.

What are some of your favorite songs?
Spend an evening once the kids are settled, and the dog is in another room with the focus on just to two of you. Turn on your favorite music and reflect on the days when your love was new. Share the blessings in your life today.

Our Musical Timeline + Playlist

Year _____ Song/ Artist _____

Memory _____

_____

_____

Year _____ Song/ Artist _____

Memory _____

_____

_____

Year _____ Song/ Artist _____

Memory _____

_____

_____

Year _____ Song/ Artist _____

Memory _____

_____

_____

Our Musical Timeline + Playlist

Year _____ Song/ Artist _____

Memory _____

_____

_____

Year _____ Song/ Artist _____

Memory _____

_____

_____

Year _____ Song/ Artist _____

Memory _____

_____

_____

Year _____ Song/ Artist _____

Memory _____

_____

_____

ABOUT THE AUTHOR

Cynthia D. Jones and her husband, Minister Quentin "Q" Jones, have been together for 50 years, married for 45 years. They are Co-founders of "Real Talk," a small group for married couples. She and Q have spoken at couples retreats, conferences, and workshops across America for 35+ years. Her goal is to mentor, encourage, and teach couples to love and grow together according to God's design for marriage. They are blessed with one son and a daughter in love. Cynthia is graduate of Alma College with a BSW.

Cynthia also has a passion for women's spiritual growth and well-being. She was a co-founder of a women's study, "Loving Him God's Way." She has served as a Bible Study Fellowship leader and volunteered with many ministries including, Hosea Feed the Hungry, Meals on Wheels, and Dress for Success. Currently, Cynthia is a Stephen Minster and is on the board of a Christian support ministry, "One Hundred Shares." Mrs. Jones has been writing for many years. *The Melody of Marriage* is her first book.

www.ingramcontent.com/pod-product-compliance
Lightning Source LLC
Chambersburg PA
CBHW050324010526
44119CB00003B/101